SHEIKH ALY N'DAW

CW01651307

LIBERATION THERAPY

Based on research conducted by
the Institute of Research
in Social and Human Sciences
for the Promotion of Peace
&
the teachings of
the School of Peace and Service
of Sheikh Ahmadou Bamba

Published 2010

French Edition 2007
Original Title: La Thérapie de Libération

Printed by Imprimerie & Papeterie Commerciale Limited
Mauritius

ISBN : 978-99949-32-17-7

Table of Contents

Chapter 1
The being that I am..1

Chapter 2
Choice - Liberty - Love..23

Chapter 3
The trap of reaction...41

Chapter 4
The meaning of life 61

Chapter 5
Forgiveness or The Science of Difference.............73

Chapter 6
The forgiveness of Peacemakers...........................93

Chapter 7
Real Life Stories...117

Conclusion...153

PRELUDE

Before starting on the subject of this work, we would like to dedicate the prelude to Maulana Siddiqui, a great Indian sage who conveyed a message of love throughout the world in the hope of uniting hearts in spite of differences, or, as we will see in the following pages, perhaps because of them.

Maulana Siddiqui said:
"In my older years, I started a trip around the world, with all the difficulties that such a trip entails, with the sole aim and mission to convey the message of peace and goodwill to other human beings, so that they may avoid conflicts and quarrels and live in harmony.

After years of deep reflection, I had come to the conclusion that the only source of human conflicts and wars resides in Man's selfishness on the one hand and Man's forgetfulness of God in relationships with other people on the other.

When people start to act in their own interests and forget their social duties, when they lower themselves to a level where they pursue only their own interests to the detriment of the rights of others, harmony and compromise fade and eventually disappear.

Thus when people are so immersed in the material world that they do not find time to remember the Creator even formally, when their relationship with the Supreme Power is cut off, when they stop understanding that by breaking the divine laws of nature, they are destroying the harmony of human existence at the same time, peace becomes impossible to attain.

We experience this in our daily lives. Every time we break the physiological laws of nature, we fall sick and suffer physical pain.

The same thing goes for the moral laws ordained by God: by breaking them, we attract only suffering. If we break somebody's heart one day, we should expect the same to happen to us the next.

Every day, every evening, you listen to music and songs on entertainment programmes on the radio. Have you asked yourself from where this melody that enthrals your heart and bewitches your ears draws so much sweetness?

When you see an orchestra, you notice that it consists of various instruments, each one with its own sounds and its own melodies. If one day the musicians decide to play independently of each other, you will hear only discordant sounds. It is only when those orchestrating the music put the different sounds of various instruments in harmony that you will find the beauty that not only captivates the audience but the musicians too.

In this way, I would like you to consider each human being as a musical instrument taking part in a concert. Learn the lesson of harmony by watching the orchestra. Remember that when you succeed in creating this harmony along with others, melodious tunes will emanate from human life, airs capable of conveying a sweetness which unfortunately belongs to days gone by. Beautiful faces and beautiful things will come to you day and night and captivate your heart. You will say that someone's face is beautiful and you will declare your love for this beauty.

I will not bore you with a talk about the nature of love on this occasion. I will perhaps tell you later on that what people call love nowadays is not love in the true sense of the word but only a name given to vulgar appetites rooted in the basest of human desires.

In truth, love means a sacred state of mind which has nothing to do with personal interest and base desires. But if you think that love is only sensual desire, I would like you to think upon this:

- Where do this beauty and grace that enthral your heart come from?
- Where do these superior differences that make you bow down come from?
- Can these material bodies become beautiful and perfect by themselves, or does a Supreme Power exist that creates this beauty and bestows these differences?

If your own nature and inner voice tell you that somebody has created the universe, so be sure that this beauty and perfection that you see in the world are only an expression of the beautiful and perfect Being that sensible people and those belonging to any religion call God.

One step further and you will be led to feel that if the beauty and perfection of things that have been created are so attractive, how much more beautiful and perfect must their Creator be!

You will allow yourself to be submerged by the beauty of things created. But I would have preferred you to focus on Him, the Being who is truly beautiful and perfect and who is the source of all life.

Think of Him, love Him. Your attitude towards love will help increase your awareness of God's omnipresence until it becomes impossible for you to act against His law.

Then you will not harm anyone and you will not break anyone's heart. Neither will you disappoint nor insult anyone. On the contrary, you will feel that black and white, rich and poor, the lowest and the highest all belong to the family of God and are therefore your own brothers and sisters.

Your love for God will enable you to inwardly love others. When you reach this state of mind, the world will finally know peace in the true sense of the word. You are used to listening to the melodies of human songs on the radio. Today you have listened to the melody of divine harmony, so from now on, think of God, and love Him with increasing devotion. From now on let us adopt superior forms of human morality.

Let us try to build *true humanity.*"

INTRODUCTION

Before beginning, we would like to reassure the reader that this book does not aim to criticise but on the contrary to provide to those who feel the need a source of reflection and a method that we have called "Liberation Therapy". Through an examination of our daily life and experiences, we can awaken our consciousness to give ourselves a chance to change and to taste true happiness.

This therapy functions as a framework that can be adapted to each individual. It provides the key that unlocks our personal histories. We just have to provide the "material" of our life story, which will act as our own personal resource in our development.

Readers will then only have to follow the

different stages of this methodology with their wonderfully clear logic and identify the particular reasons for events that have surprised or frustrated them in their daily lives. They will then be able to make the necessary changes based on true liberty and an awakened consciousness.

Liberation Therapy is a methodology that fulfils two needs:

- healing us of the diseases of the soul;
- freeing us from our mental prison.

It aims primarily to trigger a fundamental awakening of consciousness: namely, that we all live our adult lives on the basis of what we have inherited from our childhood experiences. Once this realisation has taken place and we have identified the childhood experiences that affect our adult life, the therapy will help us to free ourselves from our invisible chains and enable us to be happy at last.

Childhood is the time when we experience our first emotions. Everything we experience as children forms a type of legacy. This legacy shapes our adult life and makes us function on the basis of conclusions that we drew as a child. Such experiences may occur within a wider or narrower family circle, but they chiefly involve the king and queen of our lives in those days: our father and mother.

Naturally, we paid attention to our parents and learnt by observing the way they lived. However, like all children, we also focused on ourselves and were sensitive to what we found pleasant or unpleasant or to what we considered right or wrong according to our criteria.

Indeed, it is in childhood that we learn to judge others. When Dad shouted, we understood that it was anger and when Mum slapped us, we concluded that it was spite and we would say: "*Mum is bad, she hit me.*" We also experienced jealousy of a little brother or sister growing up by our side whom we thought was our parents' favourite. But then, when Mum gave us a sweet we would say she was nice and when Dad took us to a movie as a reward for good marks, we thought he was fair...

Such conclusions gave rise to judgement. We would declare that something was good because it gave us pleasure or that something was bad because of the displeasure we experienced...

Through this introduction to evil in particular, we were initiated to the vices (jealousy, pride, impatience...) and these vices took root within us. As adults, we form our relationships on the basis of these reference points, and we still function based on what we learnt during childhood.

In this way, our childhood was an initiation to universal vices and values. During our adulthood, this initiation must come to maturity: if we can recognise vices, we should be able to take the path of virtue. This will only be possible if we take the path that wise men and prophets such as Jesus have shown to their disciples, which will lead us to discover the "new person" within us.

To achieve this, we have to undertake work - an exercise in non-judgement and observation without evaluation. This inner work will enable us to understand that differences in all things, and in particular differences among human beings, are a basic necessity of life.

If we remain fixated by the foundations laid in our childhood - which, let's recall, were only justified by our self-centredness - then we condemn ourselves to rejecting differences in others. We'll believe that "what I do, what I like, what I believe is best – others with their tastes and habits are different from me and therefore wrong!" As each one of us in this world functions according to this pattern, we can hardly be surprised that conflicts abound between individuals, ethnic groups and nations. All of us, dominated by our own conception of what is best, try to impose it on others, with the best intentions.

Liberation Therapy will allow us to discover that our differences make us interconnected and that we complement one another. It is up to us to accept these differences and to make constructive use of them to attain a better life and to achieve happiness. They exist for this purpose. It is up to us to discover that the Earth's true wealth is the human being. Our civilisation in the third millennium must have the science of the human being as its foundation.

This book aims to throw light on this science and show that our heritage as human beings would be impoverished without these healthy differences - the human race would be poorer if the traditional skills and way of life of any one tribe, race or nation were lost.

Every aspect of creation is necessary for humanity's progress. A popular saying claims that "*Man is wolf to Man*". But Liberation Therapy shows that a liberated man is the remedy for Man, both individually and as a society.

CHAPTER 1

THE BEING THAT I AM

The founder of our school, Sheikh Ahmadou Bamba (1853-1927), was a man of great spirituality and a profound thinker. He long reflected on the nature of the human being and on the reasons which drive a person to destroy himself and his fellow beings while deep in his heart he seeks only happiness and peace.

Sheikh Ahmadou Bamba was interested in what lies at the foundation of any civilisation: the spirituality that is presumed to give meaning to Man's existence on Earth. It appeared to him that in all civilisations that he came to know, perfect unity (primarily in relation to the divine force known as God) is an absolute principle in which Man believes but which he has difficulty putting into practice with his fellow beings.

Obviously, unity on Earth would be reflected by harmony, tolerance, respect for all differences, and peace and love in all realms of human life. Each human being in his confused way aspires to a mythical Golden Age and wants to establish this ideal on Earth. But everyone thinks that this is a beautiful utopia that unfortunately *"isn't possible in this world"*.

Sheikh Ahmadou Bamba then became interested in the way the human being pledges loyalty to this unity in the last revealed religion, Islam. One who wants to take the way of perfect unity says:

"I testify that there is no other God but God."

An individual's entire commitment to the One is distilled in this formula "I testify" ("**Nash-hadou**" in Arabic), and Sheikh Ahmadou Bamba wished to explore the phrase's profound meaning.

He therefore split it into four syllables and obtained:

Na – corresponding to what can be called the carnal soul, full of desires ("nafs" in Arabic)

Sh – corresponding to what can be called "Shaytaan" – Satan and the poisoned universe

of temptations
Ha - evoking "Hawa", all the pleasures in which one can lose oneself
Dou - or "Dounya", the lower world with all the passions that alienate human beings from each other.

Thus broken up, each syllable of the word "**Nash-hadou**" corresponds to an obstacle that hinders the human soul in its search for unity.

By breaking the commitment symbolised by this key word "**Nash-hadou**", we create obstacles that prevent us realising unity, the source of happiness. It is as if unity is shattered into multiple pieces and each one of these pieces is taken for a god by deluded Man. He is then plunged in the very opposite of unity, division. He enters into a universe that is contrary to the One. The characteristics of this universe also contradict the One and this brings about conflicts, devouring ambitions and Man's destruction by Man. It is the world of vices that will lead to us becoming lost. Each vice falls into a particular category, as explained below:

1. The vices of **Na** or nafs correspond to
- bad character
- tendency to judge.

2. Those of **Sha** or Satan trigger inner or external conflicts:
- arrogance
- pride
- jealousy
- hatred.

3. Those of **Ha** or Hawa lose us under the pressure of:
- passion for this lower world
- impatience
- ostentation.

4. Lastly those of **Dou** or Dounya, in spite of the apparent innocence of this word, lead to despair.[1] These are:
- shame
- spite
- complaining.

When Man's commitment disperses into division and he maintains this division because he is fooled by the differences surrounding him, he is then lost forever, for he lives in a world of diversity: the socio-cultural, religious, political and economic environment in which we live has shaped everyone's attitudes, views and truths differently.

---

1. Translator's note: this text was originally written in French, where "doux" means "soft, gentle".

However, it is always possible to remedy this as we have received the key of "**Nash-hadou**" (the declaration that there is but the One, the Absolute and the Unique). We can always return to the fundamental unity to which we intrinsically belong and of which we are part beyond our differences.

Once our unity and the **"Nash-hadou**" are reconstituted, we are able to drive back destructive vices born of division - not by controlling them, but instead by transforming them into their opposites, the virtues. This is done in a harmonious serenity that we can call peace.

This truth conveys all the subtlety of the invaluable teaching of Sheikh Ahmadou Bamba, which allows us to begin the miraculous work on ourselves that enables us to transform our limitations into their opposites, once we have located and identified them.

It also allows us to understand the remarkable significance of the pairs of opposites on which the whole of Creation is founded. The table below juxtaposes these opposites and shows us how each of our shortcomings must be combated so that the metamorphosis can be started and accomplished.

Vices	Virtues
Arrogance	Humility
Shame	Love of truth
Vanity	Readiness to serve
Tendency to judge	Absence of judgement
Ostentation	Simplicity
Jealousy	Love
Hatred	Affection
Spite	Forgiveness
Complaining	Endurance
Passion for this world	Detachment
Bad character	Good character
Impatience	Patience

These pairs of opposites, which are at the same time the basis of harmony and the major obstacle to it, have been, as we are going to see, rooted in us since our childhood. Indeed, during our early years we may have felt that we lacked love. We will see later that this feeling introduced us to the concepts of **GOOD** and **EVIL** and made us taste the dark pleasures of such vices as jealousy, pride, judgement and spite. Childhood is the phase where our ego develops.

Our entire effort to transform ourselves will consist in overcoming this ego, that is, in crossing over to the opposite of vices and adopting the virtues that are indicated in the table above. We will put all our efforts into focusing on the opposite of these vices. It is an effort indeed because we need to overcome conditioning embedded in us since childhood, not only by the judgements that we passed on those close to us, but also by the information that these people transmitted to us. It is not easy to question our beliefs, which are after all those of our family and more widely of our social circle, our culture, and our history.

This conditioning is the soil in which these 12 vices grow, resulting in our failure to progress towards peace. We will see in the course of this book how they have established in us reflexes, habits, practices, and ways of thinking and acting which seem to be self-evidently right. But as the proverb says: "Truth lies on this side of the Pyrenees, and error beyond." One day we inevitably find ourselves confronting others who have equally strong convictions but which are opposite to ours!

In order to emerge from these apparent differences which shape our lives but which do not always tally with other cultures and beliefs, we have to leave behind our own conditioning. Only by doing this can we truly encounter others beyond our prejudices. We can hence clearly see that choosing to be de-conditioned can only be a personal choice, taken in complete liberty and committing none but the individual concerned.

The foundations of the human being

First, we have to know what kind of person we want to be: we need to know how to understand ourselves in order to become a creator of solidarity and sharing and how to discover within ourselves the ability to work with anyone. For this to happen, we have to develop a basis for relationships that allows us to relate to anyone.

Let us look at the sacred texts which inspired Sheikh Ahmadou Bamba, such as the Qur'an, and let us re-read chapter 9 verses 128-129 (*Laqad Jaa Akoum*):

"Now has come unto you a Messenger
from among yourselves, it grieves him
that you should perish, ardently anxious is he over

you, to believers is he most kind and merciful."

This text provides a clear definition of the human being. God declares that His Messenger is an ambassador among human beings, similar to them and having a father, a mother, and an uncle - a family as each one of us has. God adds:

"What you endure is hard to him.
He is full of solicitude for you; he is full of kindness and compassion towards believers."

First, how should we understand this term "believer"? "Believers" are not compared here to non-believers or atheists. Not at all! Let us consider what the Messenger affirmed - that everyone is a believer at birth. He stresses "at birth". The education imparted to the child by his parents will erase this and make the child follow one religion or another. However, in God's original concept of Man, he is a believer.

God continues to define his Messenger, whom he presents as the prototype of the human being. He says:

"He is full of kindness and compassion."

The human being, in his essence, is defined as a being of kindness and compassion. It goes without saying that Man's education grafts new elements onto his original nature that completely overshadow the kindness and compassion which give rise to love.

At the moment of Creation, God made Adam and breathed into him the four elements that shaped his spirit - kindness, compassion, love and original faith. This implies that we must recognise these in every human being. In order to do this, everyone has to first establish a relationship with himself that allows him to discover these four elements within.

When he has done that, he will realise that others are in a way multiples of himself and they also have these four elements in them. In this process we discover that we should never feel alone! We are connected to everyone else, without exception. From this perspective, we have neither friend nor enemy because whatever positive or negative emotion that another expresses on the surface, we will remain convinced, despite everything, of the love, kindness, compassion and original faith on which this person is founded.

And we must learn to collaborate not with a person's superficial, agitated emotions but with the serene foundation that constitutes his Being. If someone shows hostility, a profound lack of interest or great indifference, it should be remembered that what dwells in him is immutable and that fundamentally he is a Being of kindness, compassion, mercy and love.

It is with these intrinsic qualities that we have to collaborate. For this we have to collaborate with this truth within us. Then we will be able to establish a permanent, eternal relationship with all. We will never be disappointed because it will be eternal.

If we do not do this, any relationship will fundamentally be characterised by the law of impermanence - today we are friends and tomorrow we are rivals or enemies. The relationship itself is built on an illusion.

To escape from the law of impermanence, we need to seek out in each individual that which is eternal and establish a relationship with this aspect of him so that the relationship never changes. Such a foundation is secure, real and exists forever. Although the world and relationships are impermanent, this impermanence in fact only strengthens that which is eternal: temporary illusion exists only to reveal the eternal. And the eternal shows what is illusory and impermanent, according to the law of opposites.

We have thus discovered the foundation of positive and indestructible relationships with each and every one. Henceforth, we should not feel more comfortable with one person than with another. Why not? Because our relationship will not be founded on an illusion - it will be based on the essential reality of a person's Being constituted of the four unchanging elements. Impermanent relationships are founded on preference. Preference is by definition changeable and subject to circumstances. In a relationship between two people or groups, impermanence brings change. As a result, one person will consider that he has been betrayed by another, accusing him of not having kept his word, of not being worthy of trust. However, it is not a matter of trust - the problem is that both sides lack awareness that they have built their relationship on an illusion. Once this is understood, we see relationships with everyone as worthwhile, whether they say they are our friends or enemies. We have the profound reality of the four elements in common. In other words, there is but one Being, the Adamic Being, multiplied *ad infinitum* and diverse. But the foundation remains the same. Let us establish our relationships on this certainty - it is this that will enable us to establish relations with the whole of humanity.

Once we experience this awakening of consciousness regarding our Being, we understand that our foundation is peace, which is itself composed of the four elements that constitute the inner dignity and honour of the human being - original faith, compassion, kindness and love.

But Man has a dual nature, divine and human. He has an external dimension with four fundamental needs that he must fulfil in order to survive:

1. food
2. clothing
3. shelter
4. health and security.

The fact of satisfying these four needs makes up his external dignity and honour according to ordinary perception. We need to satisfy these needs in order to survive, and this has become the basis of all human activity.

The work of the jurist and philosopher Jeremy Bentham on the development of legal systems throws light on this subject. Bentham's philosophy originates from the principle that individuals see their interests in terms of pleasure or pain. They seek to maximise their happiness expressed by an excess of pleasure over pain. He even concludes that a law must be judged good or bad according to its capacity to increase the pleasure of all.

Driven by the urgency to satisfy his external honour and dignity, Man has today been carried away without restraint by the necessity of fulfilling these four needs. This has made him forget that the foundation of his happiness is peace and he has been pushed into the ruthless world of materialism where he runs the risk of losing his inner dignity and honour.

In this unbridled desire to preserve his dignity and honour at all costs, Man seeks to guarantee that his dignity and honour are never violated by always **HAVING**. He is then swept along by the dynamic of **HAVING** in order **TO DO** and **DOING** in order **TO BE.** This race to have more and more makes us feel that our dignity and honour depend exclusively on what we own.

All this is the product of our education and of our approach to life that has been conditioned since childhood by the three factors on which society focuses:

1. body
2. reason
3. intelligence.

Thus, when a child is born, we make sure that he is healthy and has no disabilities. His weight and growth are measured and we look after his health.

When he goes to school, he is made to develop his reason (his capability to discern) and his intelligence (his capacity to understand and to learn) by, for example, studying arithmetic, physical sciences and mathematics. He is also introduced to history and to all the social sciences for he has to develop this intelligence in a balanced manner. His identity is hence moulded so that he can enter the world of work and find a job based on his aptitudes and skills.

All this happens because our loving family believe that we should **HAVE** diplomas and a good position in society in order to be able **TO DO** great things. Our family wants us to have a wonderful career and to progress in life so that eventually we can **BE** someone significant. Without a doubt, our family loves us and wants to give us the means to live a happy life.

In his quest for happiness, the human being uses his reason to avoid suffering. In every circumstance, because of his education and conditioning, his approach to life is characterised by reason, logic and intellect.

Liberation Therapy enables him to free himself from this conditioning –the human being is far more than mere body, reason and intelligence.

He is also:

1. a heart, which is the seat of love
2. a soul (whether it is in a state of rebellion, repentance or at peace), where liberty and the potential for transformation are expressed
3. a spirit, which is directly inspired by the Divine and which, as a result, touches transcendence.

These three aspects of the Being are all fundamental but education and society often neglect them. Because of the indifference of institutions, it is solely up to the individual to develop them - they depend on him being aware.

The question of choice is therefore pertinent at this point.

We can limit ourselves to meeting the demands of society, be concerned with educating the body, reason and intelligence and be trapped in the dynamic of **HAVING** in order **TO DO** to be able **TO BE** so that *we HAVE a happy life.*

OR

We can use our sense of responsibility and commitment to start working on our heart, soul and spirit. We thus cultivate a different approach, and live in the opposite dynamic. Our priority will be **TO BE** in order **TO DO** to be able **TO HAVE** – which will be of benefit to all and will enable us **TO BE** happy.

What difference is there between these two options?

- "**Having a happy life**" is a precarious choice since it makes us depend on external factors such as wealth and the attitude of others, and we are vulnerable to their caprices and changes.

- "**Being happy**" frees us from this precarious state of affairs. Attainment of a "happy life" is not out of the question, but we are not dependent on it.

Peace cannot be experienced in any other way; we have to "be the peace that we want to see" in order to be happy and give happiness and peace to others. The diagram on the next page illustrates this concept.

The essential elements of this inner transformation are emergence from the family circle with its reference points, ways of behaving,

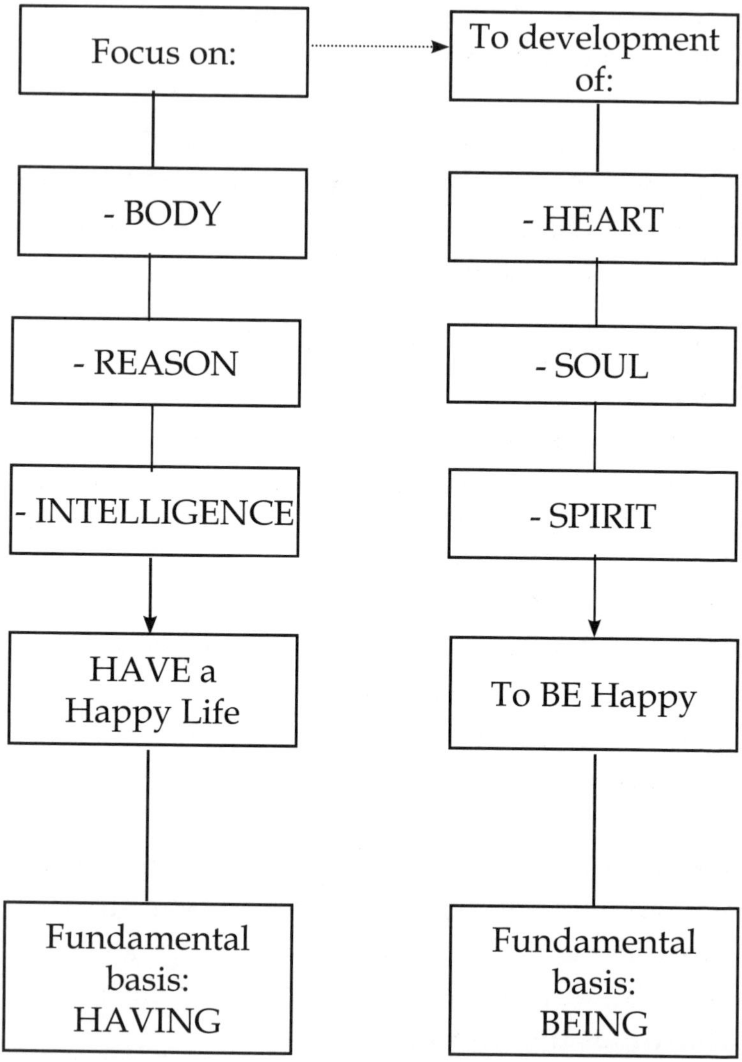
Focus on:
- BODY
- REASON
- INTELLIGENCE
HAVE a Happy Life
Fundamental basis: HAVING
To development of:
- HEART
- SOUL
- SPIRIT
To BE Happy
Fundamental basis: BEING

characteristics and conception of good and evil and the fact of opening ourselves up to a wider universe which is far more stimulating and exalting. It is the universe of the global family.

This huge family with its diverse components, cultures, languages, and customs has only one requirement for anyone who wants to belong to it – that they stop judging!

We human beings exist in a world which shows, through all its opposites, that the diversity that surrounds us is truly a life force.

Life's dynamism comes from opposites: through night we discover the light of day, illness allows us to appreciate health, age makes us value youth, and youth permits us to enjoy the unacknowledged serenity of old age... From the concepts of opposites, spring the dynamism and energy for life.

A human being bases his life on this duality, on these pairs of opposites. He tries to give life meaning based on his values. But he remains divided between his ideal and his daily reality. He is torn between what is and what should be. Naturally it is difficult for him to find a balance, a middle way that will allow him to live in peace and happiness.

He thus lives life trapped in a self that sways like a pendulum which changes the focus of his interests, from month to month, day to day, and one minute to another. What fascinated him yesterday suddenly becomes meaningless for him today. Once a passion is forgotten, he seeks to give meaning to his life in the discovery and love of new things. Deep within him, he maintains his hope for a new society, the Golden Age which will bring this illusory world to an end.

But who believes in this new world profoundly enough to make it a reality?

"No change, No chance"

Let's say it here and now: it is impossible to change anything in our environment if we keep the same mindset and behaviour. The proverb is right: no change, no chance.

It is inner change that awakens consciousness. This awakening is the most difficult process in Liberation Therapy: it occurs only when there is a break with the present or rather with the illusions of the present. Once this awakening takes place, illusions retreat into the past where they belong. Through this break and awakening to reality, it is possible to see the nature of our actions clearly, for knowledge emerges with this new awakening.

How can we achieve this awakening? Is there a magic answer to this question? Alas! Such an answer does not exist. We can however be certain that the answer will not come from the external world or from the areas of socio-economics or socio-religion. What is happening in these spheres foretells the Apocalypse. We cannot do anything on such a basis!

We have to learn the lesson that *we can do better than just doing something*!

DOING involves being dependent on having certain resources to attain our ends, and as long as we believe that our ability to act depends on these resources, our capacity to **BE** will remain fictitious, appearing and disappearing according to whether we have the means of doing anything or not. Let us not wait for the means to reach our ends. Let us be committed to ridding ourselves of all anger, of all desire to compete and of our inferiority and superiority complexes. When we are fully free from all this, we will know exactly who we are and consequently, what we want.

CHAPTER 2

CHOICE - LIBERTY - LOVE

When we are born into human society, none of us possesses anything. But society is convinced that it is necessary **TO HAVE** in order **TO DO** to be able **TO BE** someone

The awakened person will seek **TO BE** first. Thus is born the Being who depends on no-one and nothing except his personal commitment to transform himself. This means that he takes responsibility for the consequences of his actions - for what he does will inevitably lead to consequences. The actions of the Being of Peace will, of course, enable him to **HAVE**. But he will not run the risk of being conditioned by **HAVING** for he is already committed to action. He has started by **BEING**, and hence he is neither afraid of nor dependent on others' opinion. He also does not depend on outside events or circumstances. He is therefore in complete control of his **HAVING.**

All spiritual masters and advisers seek to help us discover this Being within ourselves. Those of us who can follow in their footsteps and succeed in mastering **HAVING** rather than beings its slaves, develop into true Beings of Peace and are, we can say, real benefactors of humanity.

But we can reach this stage only by using our own experiences for we are each our own resource for learning. We see in this book that it is our childhood that introduces us to universal values. Each one of us is called upon not to **oppose** our previous way of being by confronting or controlling it, but instead to become a Being in the prophetic sense, an awakened being, through **self-transformation**.

What is the outcome of the action of awakened beings? In our hierarchical society those who have nothing find themselves at the bottom of the social scale. The achievement of Beings of Peace is to make these marginalised people, the lowest in the social stratum, leaders of a new society. Thus they prove that we can reach better and quicker results than the State with its legal, social and medical institutions…

They are perceived as troublemakers who question the traditional values of society. They are attacked and persecuted. Two groups confront each other: those upholding traditional values and those who follow the Beings of Peace. However, if the former reject and fight against the latter, those who follow Beings of Peace are not caught up in a pair of opposites - that is only how it appears. As we have seen, the darkness seems to oppose the light, but actually it is thanks to darkness that we can know what light and its effects are. It is in this way that Beings of Peace bring harmony between apparent opposites.

Let us take the example of Jesus in the Gospel. He says:

"You learned what has been taught. You will love your neighbour and hate your enemy. But I say to you, love your enemies, bless those who curse you, do good to those who hate you and pray for those who ill treat you and persecute you so that you will be the son of your Father who is in the heaven for He causes his sun to rise on the evil and the good, and sends rain on the righteous and the unrighteous (…)"

(Matthew – 5: 43-48).

It is very important to understand Jesus' message in this text. He shows that we should not be trapped by the principle of opposites, between good and evil, between the saint and the scoundrel. We must avoid being trapped by words. In his model of relationships, Jesus follows the formula of **BEING** in order **TO DO** to be able **TO HAVE** which leads to total harmony and true love whereas **TO HAVE** in order **TO DO** to be able **TO BE** generates division.

How easy and pleasant it is to congratulate ourselves, to say fine words and utter pious sentences, but how difficult it is to adopt this attitude with our "enemies"!

Jesus and his disciples were no longer trapped by the principle of opposites. They had reached harmony and were in a state of action. This action was not dictated by the enemy; they did not consider others as their enemy. It therefore was not reaction. True love is not put into practice by empty words but by action!

If we manage to get to this stage, the very fact that we are putting true love into practice frees us from our enemies for we let go of the very concept. Our actions remove the word from our vocabulary. But if there is no action, we remain in the dynamic of words, and cannot change the world. We can explore all the theories on the planet but if action does not follow, theories will always remain mere dogma.

Escaping from the trap of words enables us to reach the middle way. The middle way is where love can emerge between those who love and those who do not love. When one is in the middle way, one is not in the pair of opposites any more. This is true love.

When we have been able to escape from this trap, we are no longer dominated by the past and by the sufferings experienced in situations long over but which are so painful that they awaken old behaviours that weigh on our conscience. On the contrary, we are firmly rooted in the present moment and we escape from the poverty of reaction. We can find a type of peace and we become the prime mover in our own life and a force in society.

This is the inner peace to which the messengers of peace call us and which enables us to become a Being of Peace. A person who follows the middle way is a benefactor of humanity. We only have to make this choice, for each one of us has this potential.

We hence understand that imitating the prophets and saints does not mean copying their external practices but putting into practice our capacity to follow this path, their path. The saints, prophets and Beings of Peace are in the dynamic of action in society and this causes their opponents to react. However, what is reaction? It is an attitude that corresponds to a need, a desire to protect ourselves against something that could destroy us.

It is at this point that the notion of true choice appears. It arises from the law of opposites, the law of duality. We are always faced with at least two options: good or evil, darkness or light, heat or cold. We are confronted with two realities, one of which must destroy the other to survive. And at this point, the question arises: will we accept or not the consequences of our choice whatever they are. All the liberators of the heart have faced similar situations.

In order to make a decision when faced with pairs of opposites, we need a will. This will is shown in our efforts to extricate ourselves from the nature of our society. It is shown in our personal commitment.

How is this will expressed? Generally, when we want something, it is because we love it.

We devote ourselves totally to it. It is this that makes us capable of achieving our will - love vests our will with power.

If someone was to suddenly ask you what your dearest wish and aspiration was, you might be caught off guard. You would feel that such a question requires reflection. It is first of all necessary to know what you want to make a choice and as a result put your liberty into practice.

Liberty implies that if we commit ourselves to action, others are not compelled to follow. We should not reason that "*Whoever loves me should follow me*" or "*Those who follow me are my friends and if they don't follow me, they are my enemies.*" This would be to embark on a relationship that excludes liberty, a relationship of violence.

At this stage, we have to be quite conscious that our free choices commit only ourselves. Indeed, no Being of Peace has ever compelled anyone to follow him. Instead, people see him act and realise that his actions correspond to their reality and to who they are. Hence they follow him. This fact of not imprisoning anybody in our actions and allowing everyone the possibility to choose freely means that we respect their liberty. Liberty cannot be exercised in the absence of choice.

It is the ability to choose that enables the human being to both fulfil his external plans and reach inner fulfilment. When we are faced with two opposing realities, we must make a choice. In other words, our lives lead us to the awareness that at every moment, we are steering between two extremes: we can either be agents of unhappiness or agents of happiness.

Choice does not mean that we should choose the person who best corresponds to our aspirations or who promises to fulfil our hopes, as in presidential elections. What we call choice is above all the stance we take in relation to fundamental issues: the meaning we want to give to our life, the changes we want to see in society, and the situations we refuse to see continuing. This choice implies once again consciousness of our responsibility and our readiness to assume the consequences of the actions determined by our choice.

Free choice does not consist of saying *"I prefer this to that"* for in this case we are still acting according to what pleases us most and not based on a real choice that implies giving up all other considerations. Preference always involves the consideration of differences and when such differences are taken into account, conflicts will inevitably arise.

This is the story of our relationships with others. Most of the time, whatever we do, we justify ourselves by making others responsible for what displeases us or for the world's misfortunes. We do not see what we can change and we feel free from all responsibility. When we have truly understood what a choice freely made is, our attitude changes. To overcome violence, we need to embody peace.

This is what has made people who were initially unexceptional become so famous. Let us take the example of Gandhi. Nothing would have distinguished this ordinary lawyer from his scores of colleagues or even from the crowds of Indians of the 20th century. What made him such a legendary, mythical figure? The fact that he was able at a crucial moment of his life to make a free choice for justice out of love for his people. And from this moment, nothing was ever the same in his life.

Having made a free choice in complete consciousness, he agreed to go to prison, to risk his life and to make all the commitments necessary to put an end to everything that he saw reproduced around him. In less than a lifetime, by virtue of a choice to which Gandhi had committed his life, he liberated millions of people in the Indian sub-continent who had been in bondage for a century.

We see then that through action (such as that of Gandhi, for example, when he revolutionised the Indian economy with his spinning wheel) not only can we live in the present moment but we can produce a process of **HAVING** that generates solidarity and sharing. This type of having makes it possible for any individual to work with others, no matter whom. This is possible through relationships established by a Being who is respectful of the differences of all and who, in the midst of all these differences, makes no distinction whatsoever.

When we consider the actions of Gandhi, Martin Luther King, William Penn, and Sheikh Ahmadou Bamba, we can understand that nonviolence is not simply the opposite of violence. It is much more than that: it is the foundation of a nation of peace. A nation of peace is not made by a law on a sheet of paper. It is achieved by the formation of Beings who make up this nation. It is these Beings who embody peace. We should therefore firstly devote ourselves to the formation of Beings who incarnate peace. Such was the work of the prophets.

All the difficulty resides in the fact that individuals function according to reference points to which they always return. This is the source of conflicts. The one who makes no distinction between differences is the source of peace. He is hence firmly rooted in action and not in reaction.

Like Gandhi, Sheikh Ahmadou Bamba, the prophets and the saints, the one who can become a Being of Peace, a benefactor of humanity, must understand that one should make differences a necessity of life, not a cause for killing others, scorning them and creating wars in order to exist in a relationship characterised by domination.

We can see that if we achieve this, we no longer criticise nor judge: we have been able to escape from the trap of words. To achieve this, we must BE. Such a choice is not possible without the inner liberty that releases us from the outer opinion of others. Love, in this context, is the driving force of our liberty. It guides our choices. It inspires our heart, the seat of divine light, which impels our life.

Whatever our profound nature, whether it generates disorder or order around and within us, it is impossible to avoid the conclusion that we radiate only what we are, not what we say, think or feel with our senses, but merely what we are. It is therefore essential for every one of us to know who he is and where he is.

Isn't humanity's situation today the result of the sum of our thoughts first and foremost, and then of our actions? Haven't we always been stuck in our attitudes and behaviour, so that all our abilities and potential have only served to lead us to our current plight, an era of endless wars?

However, even if we have the potential to destroy, we also have the capacity and potential to change. It is a question of going back to our original nature, which at a very deep and intimate level is made up of kindness, compassion, love and original faith, so that we can transform our inner chaos and create order.

Thus we will see the light of peace emerging through the one who has restored balance within himself and found the middle way. This individual will have the mission of representing the divine will on earth and unconditional love. In short, it means a return to the natural relationship with the Absolute through the "natural" religion in which Man was destined by God to live and in which he was born, before his parents moulded him to fit the shape of religious institutions (whether Islam, Christianity, Judaism, Hinduism, and so on). We should not forget that etymologically the word "religion" comes from "re-ligere", "to connect" - true religion connects Man to the Absolute, without boundaries and borders.

Each child is born in original faith - this sense of the Absolute and an aspiration to the transcendence of love, beauty and peace. It is only later that his parents make him the follower of one religion or another. As we grow up, as our life unfolds, our precious inner life becomes populated with the false gods of our daily lives. They fill us with gloom and darkness instead of bringing light to us. As we have seen, they bear such names as arrogance, jealousy, envy, hatred, and spite....

Thus, we have to take care of our inner life by striving to drive away these shadows of our true selves. When we get rid of them, we rid ourselves of influences which are external to our lives and are often so mutually contradictory. We will hence find inner liberty and cease using their attributes (arrogance, jealousy, envy, hatred, and wickedness) which lead us into an infernal spiral from one increasingly violent reaction to the next.

Who does not remember riots in the suburbs against which squads of policemen are sent? What happens the next day? More and more rioters come back! If more police vans are deployed, all the city's suburbs are soon set ablaze.

However, working to free our inner life from the influence of and dependence on external events will enable us to escape from this terrible law of cause and effect. We will become free with a true internal liberty that cannot be touched by external turbulence.

Then, we will be imbued and guided by love. We will metamorphose into Beings of Peace, humanity's true benefactors, inhabited by everlasting peace which can be spread all around.

What about Love?

Let us say at once that love is not what is merely expressed in words, it is a truth that must be put into practice. The famous words "*I love you, you love me*" have nothing to do with the love that we are talking about here.

Love is the sum of generosity, compassion, and self-dedication. We have seen the 12 virtues taught by Sheikh Ahmadou Bamba (page 6); the sum of these virtues makes up "love".

We have once again to be careful of the trap of words in a society based on reaction. In this society, when we report favourably on a person and say for example that he has been generous, it is because he has rendered a service to us. Everything is seen in relationship to ourselves. To know if he is truly generous, we have to know whether he would have acted in the same way with another person!

If we say that another person is patient, again it is in relationship to ourselves. We do not know if he would have been with someone else. If he likes the look of me, he will be patient but if he does not, he will be the complete opposite. We are therefore completely caught up in the principle of action and reaction.

We have all had this experience on countless occasions. If we take the example of people who have just visited a government office, we see that their opinion about the counter clerks differs in every respect. On any occasion when someone is being discussed, two opinions will be given. This is because the person concerned has taken a different attitude towards the two speakers.

Our analysis of others in fact reflects our shortcomings and our needs in terms of affection and feelings. Everything we say about others expresses our own need. It is so strong in us that if we hear people talking for the first time about a person whom we do not know at all, we firmly believe what the person we know is saying. Why is this so? It is because it answers our needs.

However, to be in a position to judge objectively whether someone is truly kind, we ourselves have to embody kindness. If we ourselves are not truly kind, our assessment is not founded on real knowledge but on our own shortcomings and needs.

We have to love ourselves as we are. We need to know that we have the potential to be a benefactor of humanity but the most important thing is to know that we need to **BE**.

A person conditioned by **HAVING** will not reach this state of being a benefactor to humanity. As long as he remains conditioned by **HAVING**, he will think that if he does not have, he will be in danger of disappearing. We only have to look at the US and its need for oil - without oil, it would not exist any more. It needs oil in order to be. We all know the tragic consequences of this.

HAVING is at the root of all our conflicts.

Nothing is bad in itself. Materialism in itself is not bad. However, we are ignorant of ourselves. Just imagine! How can we believe that we must have in order to be? When our knowledge is so poor, all our self-knowledge is poor. Little importance is given to the self. We can be among the wealthiest people in the world, possess all the gold of the Earth and enjoy high status but one day, all this will go to other people. On that day, we will not exist any more. Our possessions are not aware of who owns them!

My Master used to tell me:

"You must love something that can respond to your love. Anything else that you love will destroy you and will not bring you back to life."

For example, someone who loves cigarettes gives all his money, health and everything else to them. Cigarettes kill this person and do not make him come back to life. This is what it is like to love something that does not respond to your love and to love inanimate objects.

Love is to give yourself completely to what you love. Then you discover another dimension of love which gives life. It is a love that takes you away from pairs of opposites and leads you to the middle path. This is the prerogative of the True Being, the one who masters **HAVING** and who makes use of it in a non-selfish way. It is the prerogative of the Being who excludes none as he makes no distinction between differences and who, as we have seen, makes it possible for each to work with all.

The key to peace is not to distinguish between differences, which comes about through work on the self. Choice, liberty and love are the three elements that form the Being of Peace. When one of these elements is missing, the person becomes conditioned and goes back to reaction. And reaction positions him in the past, always lagging behind the present moment.

Choice and liberty are the elements that will enable love to be born. In the absence of these two conditions, love is a mere word. We need to experience choice and liberty to experience love in action.

CHAPTER 3

THE TRAP OF REACTION

From America to the depths of Oceania, everyone finds themselves facing the same relationship problem: the problem of **BEING**.

To understand the phenomenon better, let us return to the family unit. We grew up among our relatives, or at least among adults who brought us up, and who introduced us to relationships with others.

When a child is brought into the world, because of his weakness and his parents' ardent desire for him to be healthy, the baby will draw his first conclusions about his role and the role of others in his life. He notices that he can demand food and it is brought to him. He can also get food that he likes and refuse what he does not like, be in the arms of his mother all the time, and satisfy his desire for affection and need for comfort and physical well-being. His parents, on their side, have an absolute duty to satisfy him at every moment. For the baby, such is the world: he has all the rights and his parents have all the duties!

And throughout this relationship with our parents and family (grandparents, uncles, aunts, cousins, brothers, sisters and even family pets), we are initiated to the concept of good and evil or rather to "what is good for me, what is bad for me; what pleases me and what displeases me." This initiation enables us to form an **IDEAL**, which we firmly believe will be the basis for a happy life in future.

As our quest for happiness is a human experience, we have the tendency to remember the "inhuman" aspect of our experiences (lack of love, loneliness, ill treatment, abandonment...) to make sure that we do not experience these in our future relationships with others. When shaping our ideal of life, we base ourselves on the "inhuman" aspect of our experiences with our parents and we express our wish simply thus:

"I will do everything in order not to go through what my parents experienced".

If we have first experienced the pangs of terror with our father or mother, we set ourselves the objective of being their exact opposite. Whether we are a man or woman, we joyfully imagine a partner who conforms to our wishes and enables us to avoid reliving our childhood experiences. Hence, our ideal is entirely drawn from our parents' conjugal life.

As part of this ideal, we see ourselves as the prototype of the ideal man or woman, based on our experiences in our family. We only have to find the ideal partner, who naturally must not resemble the person who caused us so much suffering in our family. We will see that this is completely based on our experiences with our parents and is a product of our past.

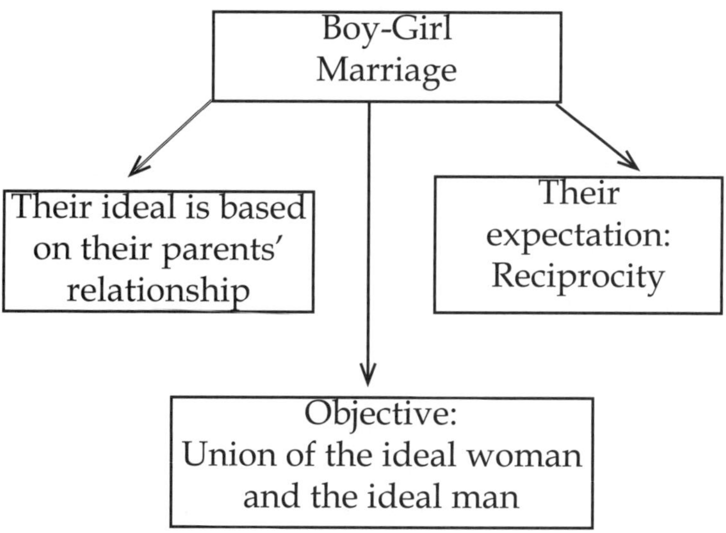

We have condemned and judged these past experiences. We have positioned ourselves as victims. Our ideal will inevitably be founded on a reaction to this past.

What shape will this reaction take? It will be to turn to the outside world to look for an ideal partner who can ensure that we will never again relive the painful experiences of our past. This partner will permit us to escape from living with someone whom we have judged in our childhood family and will prevent us from re-experiencing such difficulties in our personal life. We therefore look for the opposite of the person we have criticised. But as we have judged him or her, we will always be trapped in the role of victim and still fully connected to the events of the past. Against our will, we start a quest for a person who will allow the same childhood pattern to be reproduced in order to enable us to play the role that we want. This is a choice born from reaction and not from action.

Our intimate relationships are, without us being aware of it, more a means of filling the emotional voids resulting from our history of relationships within our family than encounters based on true love. What is the result? Well, we reproduce exactly what we wanted to avoid and in the same conditions!

As days and months pass after her marriage, a girl realises that the man she has married is a reproduction of her own father, and that she herself, without having noticed it, has become a reproduction of her mother!

So, disappointed by what they see as a failure, saddened by their inability to achieve the ideal life of their dreams, husband and wife look for a new means to escape from their inevitable fate. This time, they will focus on the future and seek to be reborn through the birth of their children. In this way a new cycle of reproduction begins as the parents remain in the framework of reaction, and in this framework, as we have seen, there is no possibility of making a real choice. There is no liberty. It is hence useless to speak of love!

Their child will be born. He or she will be a third member of their relationship, resulting in a shift that places the child at its heart.

Paul's Story

Like everyone else, Jacques and Chloe have formed their relationship on the basis of childhood experiences. They have just had a child, a cute little boy called Paul. What happens after the great joy of the first days? As is always the case in a relationship between two people, as soon as a third member appears, this first relationship will be reconstructed – that is part of the essence of relationships.

Paul finds himself at the heart of this relationship between his father and his mother, as an observer. He listens to and watches what is said and done. He watches the relationship between his father and mother.

Unfortunately, the ideal that led his parents, Jacques and Chloe, to get married was an illusion. They inevitably reproduce the behaviour of their own fathers and mothers, according to what they have experienced in their childhood.

Paul keeps observing them. He observes how they relate to each other, what they say to each other, what happens firstly between them and then between his mother and himself and between his father and himself. He learns to recognise and experience emotions, to feel the weight of words and the harm caused by them. He hears what his parents say to each other, then what his mother tells his father about him and what he hears his father say about him.

What he hears and experiences most often comes down to either criticism or praise - they are a pair of opposites too!

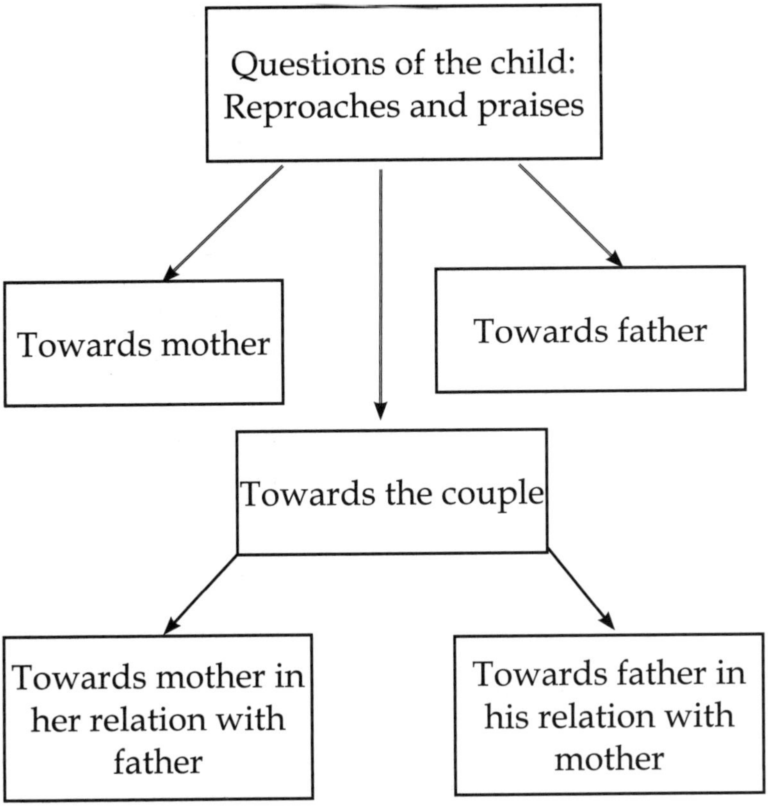

Paul is introduced to all relationships through this first relationship. Even at this stage, he starts identifying the victim in these conflicts – mother or father? In most cases, it is this mother, so he immediately sides with her. He may also see the victim as his father, although this is rarer. In this case he sides with his father.

What happens then?

Paul grows up in this situation. At times, he expects support from his mother because of his father's attitude towards him. Sometimes she fails him by not taking his side. Sometimes it is the contrary: his father does not come to his aid and Paul finds him wanting. In some circumstances, Paul condemns them both.

As years pass, Paul makes a sort of assessment of his family relationships. His experience will gradually shape his own ideal of a couple. When he becomes an adult, he will emerge from the family circle. He will not be empty-handed - he will carry with him his family relationship legacy and his own evaluation of it in terms of its successes and failures.

Thus, this family legacy will lead him:

- either to condemn his father because he sees his mother as a victim of his father's behaviour;
- or to condemn his mother as responsible for his father's behaviour;
- or purely and simply to condemn both parents because of the way he sees them as a couple.

But he may also have a feeling of veneration for

both parents. Such veneration could have as its source:
consciousness, or
alienation.

Conscious veneration is the rational respect that we give our parents because they have done extraordinary things or they have displayed great qualities. We are proud of them. We worship our parents for their courage in a particular situation, for their sharp intelligence that led them to make such-and-such a discovery... they do not have to be famous; it is sufficient that they have aroused our admiration or that of people around us. "My dad was the greatest hunter in the village" or "People were always asking my mum for her jam recipes. Nobody could do it the way she did." Such aspects of the parents' daily lives can arouse conscious veneration in their children.

Veneration by alienation makes a child say: "I always saw my parents doing it like this, so I do it this way too!" If you ask him why, he will answer: "My parents did it this way. That's the way it is and that's that!"

The child assesses his parents as a couple as follows:

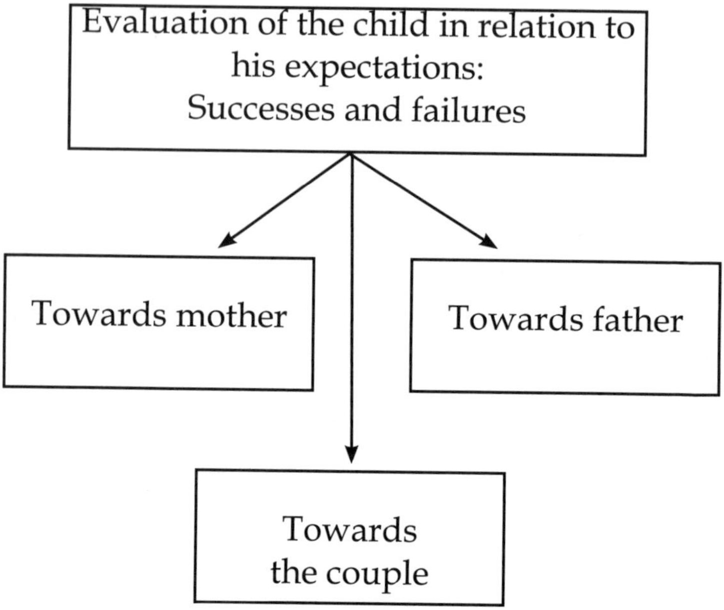

And now the child emerges from his family circle, endowed with all these relationship experiences and aspirations for his future. He feels convinced that he can at last make his own choices based on the ideal that he has conceived. But as we clearly see, his state of being is based on his judgement and condemnation of his parents, and so he is entirely inhabited by his past. He therefore does not have a real choice and consequently, he does not have an ideal.

He will therefore do the opposite of what he condemned his parents for, telling himself that he will never reproduce what he has experienced until then.

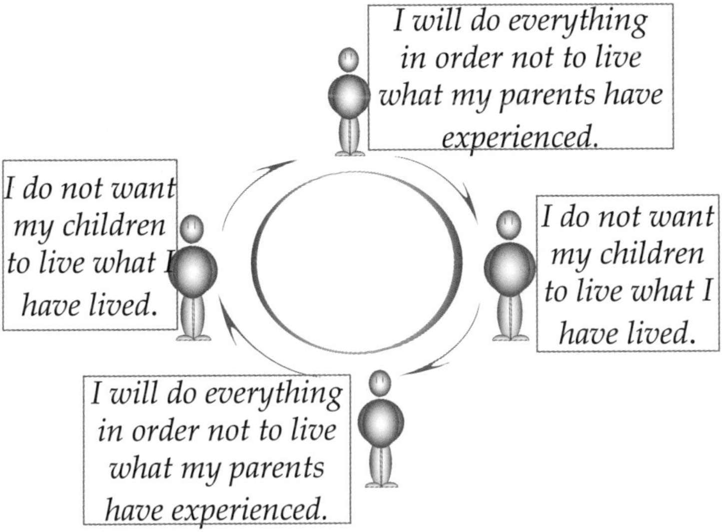

He is in a state of reaction and to justify it, he needs to act in such a way that his actions (similar to those of his parents) trigger a reaction similar to his reaction as a child. Thus, if he has criticised his father, he will need to find a wife who will allow him to justify this criticism. He will seek a wife, quite unconsciously, likely to enter into a dynamic of reaction with him. He will inevitably find a girl with these characteristics, which will enable him to find in her his ideal. He will recognise her as ideal without realising for one single moment that she is in fact a reflection of his own mother.

Why does this vicious circle, this trap, exist? In the diagram above, you will see that the individual does not take any initiative or action concerning his life and his future. He is not in control of his life; he is always squeezed between his past and his present. He does not live in the present moment. He does not seek reference points within himself and based his own ideas but from his painful past. He conceives his future only in relationship to his past.

His past is made up of regret, anger, hatred, jealousy and rejection. His future frightens him because when he imagines a future based on his past, he does not know what will become of him and he is afraid.

He will spend his life oscillating between a past characterised by anger, jealousy, and hatred (sometimes going even to the point of rejecting humankind) and an uncertain future. Living between the past and the future, a past where his plans failed and that was marked by vices and a future he knows nothing about, what can he experience in the present moment apart from doubt? He will be dependent on alliances and affections of every description… This individual has lost his bearings and is reproduced in generation after generation.

His present moment is spent blaming circumstances and people in his past. He does not hold himself accountable for his failures because he is convinced that if his life plan (that he developed unconsciously, based on his history) has not succeeded, it is because of those who did not pay attention to his aspirations. Whatever happens to him is the fault of others and they have to pay. Seen from this point of view, he is a victim from every angle and he sees everyone else as oppressors. He looks in his close environment for those responsible for his failures and condemns them to make sure that all of this does not re-occur.

The point of entry to this circle is judgement. This circle places us in a constant state of judgement. When we judge, we stick labels on everyone and leave the human dimension: people are no longer seen as human beings, they are defined and reduced to the labels they have been given. *"This one is like this, that one is like that..."* We cannot avoid this deviation if we seek to give meaning to our lives based on our childhood experiences.

The fact is that at the very moment when we judge and condemn, we allow the 12 vices to reign supreme in our heart. Our refusal to take responsibility will have the deadly consequence of creating chaos within and around us. All our relationships are distorted and we are led directly to a process of repetition. Let us recall that all this has sprung from our initial resolution: *"I don't want to do anything based on that because I didn't like it"*. This thought inspires and directs us; it controls and drives us. Filled with this thought, how can we fail to reproduce a past that forms part of our being? This shows the power of ideas and thoughts.

This pattern means that we are inspired by a past that we hate but that which dominates our inner selves, and we cannot help but drag it into our present and reproduce through our actions the person we condemned in the past. The trap of reaction is hermetically sealed!

The problem is to know how to emerge from this situation. Let us repeat: while he remains unconsciously trapped in his legacy, the individual is not in a situation to make a choice.

Resolving our relationship legacy

Knowing who we are! Knowing what we want! To achieve this, we have to free ourselves from the illusions that we have harboured since our childhood and that cause us to function rather than to live. Such is the help that Liberation Therapy will bring to those who wish it…

And speaking of love, let us talk about marriage. The preceding chapter shows how difficult it is to make a success of our married life based on the usual foundations. The number of marriages ending in divorce proves how true this is. Each week, couples unite for better and for worse. They start with the better but when the worse comes, there is a change in direction. They do not stand in front of a white-cassocked priest but in front of the black-robed judge. We leave it to the judge in his courtroom to rule on the end of the marriage that we had initially dreamt of creating in quite another place.

Before the judge, each party recites a long list of all the harm that the other has caused him throughout their married life. But when he is asked about the good that he has received, he finds nothing to say. Nothing is left! It would seem that this couple has spent 20 to 30 years of their life harming each other! As if there has not been a single moment of happiness between them! Is there better proof of what they felt for each other? Love, it would seem, never existed!

Therefore, right from the beginning of married life, our relationship is distorted. We have a false idea of love, a false idea of the words that we utter, which do not represent reality but which illustrate our shortcomings and emotions. We say: "This person is nice", but in reality this is because we think her or she can fulfil one of our needs. We are not aware of this need at first but we feel that this person touches something within us, so we attribute a quality to him or her and say: "*He is nice*" or "*She is so gentle*".

Almost all unions are founded on no more than an aspiration to fill emotional gaps created in childhood. When the child grows up and leaves his family to start his own, he is still trapped in the reality of a 15-year-old and still guided by the principle of reaction. He will choose his partner and even if for official purposes he is 20 or 30 years old, he will behave like a 15-year-old for this is the age when he underwent the experiences that he would carry with him when he left the family circle.

If we look closely, we can see that regardless of our age, whether we are 30, 40, or 50, each of us has the state of mind of a 15-year-old and acts as he does. Such is the complex nature of the judgement which trapped us in the moment when we uttered it and shaped our ideal.

Parents recognise themselves in their teenage child – he is 15 and we are 40 or 50 but we have the strange feeling that we are growing up in front of ourselves. We are confronted with the consequences of the judgements we passed long ago.

Our observations (who in the family is nice or good, and who is not) taught us the 12 vices that we needed to know in order to make judgements. But while we thought we were condemning others, we were actually condemning ourselves for the judgement forced us to repeat what we wanted to escape from…

So, how can we escape from this trap? We have seen that we cannot stop the process merely by repeating "I am not going to start it again – I do not want to reproduce my history…" for the minute we say this, we are in a state of judgement. And if we condemn, we reproduce!

We therefore have to leave judgement behind and not allow ourselves to be guided by it. It must not be allowed to condition our actions.

How can we do this? Let us recapitulate. We leave our family circle convinced that we are free at last, that we can make choices and experience love. We even believe that we have an ideal based on our past where we have validated what we called "good" and condemned what we have called "bad".

However, a true ideal does not lead us to condemn others! It can only be concluded that in fact, we do not have an ideal when we join human society with all our shortcomings and vices born of judgement and *we build our relationships with other people on a flawed basis!* It is this person whom we are, embodying the 12 vices mentioned above, who will establish relationships with others! Let us imagine what the results will be! The whole reproduction phenomenon will start all over again!

The main question is: **How do we transform our family relationship legacy so that it allows us to join the global family not by reproducing what we experienced but by improving upon it?**

Now it is time for us to go further and examine how to resolve our legacy!

We have seen that the child draws his ideal from the married life of his parents. He says to himself: "*My parents are a perfect couple; I absolutely want to follow their example*" or he thinks: "*My parents went through hell; I'll do everything I can to avoid going through all that in my personal life."*

When one day, a boy and a girl meet and realise that their concepts of the ideal partner correspond, the "marriage" of two ideals will lead to the marriage of the two people. But actually, it will be a relationship where each tries to find a solution to the emotional gaps left by their childhoods.

The couple then unconsciously establish a new relationship "pact" where each will check if the other is obeying the (tacit) commitments that he or she has supposedly made. The other partner will do the same. So instead of founding their married life on mutual trust, they will constantly be watching each other and asking *"is he (or she) fulfilling my justifiable expectations of a partner?"*

However, all the factors leading to this new relationship pact result from our concept of the ideal. This ideal has been manufactured from the experiences we had within the family environment where we grew up. We produce and fix our concept of the ideal on the basis of the relationship between our father and mother and the relationship that we had with each of them. It is the events that we have witnessed, heard, and undergone that bring us, once we reach marriageable age, to feel close to the partner of our dreams, a partner who corresponds to our perception of our ideal life.

Why? Because we need to distribute roles so that we can embody or make others embody an individual whose actions we condemned in our childhood.

So, if we condemned our father's violence, we are filled with this memory and cannot avoid playing the role of the violent father. But for this to happen, we need to find a wife who will allow us to do this. This wife must have a character and legacy that will enable us to justify and to express our judgement and condemnation of our father.

Before going further, let us make clear that the fact of an individual's siding against one of his parents has more impact on his behaviour than the alternative of siding with one of them.

Chapter 4

THE MEANING OF LIFE

There is much talk of giving meaning to life. We think that life requires us in order to have meaning. But life itself is an act of love of God, who wishes to illustrate this love through the human being! To experience life is to experience this love.

By wanting to give life a sense, we are rejecting this love and only seeing life from our own narrow point of view. To do this, we make use of differences among ourselves and emphasise three areas that dominate our reality: culture, religion and the economy. Many communities and people try to give a meaning to life based on differences.

A good example is apartheid in South Africa. The white community tried to give meaning to its life by relying on one difference, race. It therefore used cultural and religious values, based on religion and the economy, to support apartheid and their outlook. Other people use linguistic criteria, still others apply purely cultural criteria.

But when we do this, we are no longer trying to give meaning to life. Instead, we are trying to use these three areas to justify our nature, which is based on our family relationship legacy.

Let's take religion for example. A substrate of culture and religious practices has built up behind the message. Religion mingles with the culture of the places to which it spreads. We hear people speaking about Indian, African or European Islam! Yet the reference point is the same - the Qur'an. However, in our present societies, religion is experienced through these three factors (culture and religious practices, themselves based on the economy) that give a false impression of unity of religious experience and distort our understanding of faith.

On the other hand, there are those who oppose religion and say they are atheists. When we speak about religion to them, they say: "*Above all, I am a human being."* Well, they seem more advanced than religious people because they are aware that they are human beings above all! They are right. This is an important point, as all faiths give priority to the human being. If the messages of the prophets and saints had been limited to meditation or chants, there would have been no problem. But it is our humanity that is at the heart of their message, touching us directly.

If the objective of Moses, for example, had simply been to build synagogues and to spend his time in front of the Wailing Wall, the Pharaoh would not have been worried. But Moses wanted to free humans from the yoke around their necks so that they would achieve self realisation.

All divine messages without exception have related to the question of being. This shows once again that God's message is above all a religion of being. Let us remember *"that which we love most and for which we give up all else is our true god"*, so that apart from the god we worship in religious temples, each has his god who determines truly what he does and for which he gives up everything else.

This is seen in assemblies and meetings. We

have the intention of doing something good together and everyone comes. But as soon as the activity starts, it can be seen that some people withdraw into themselves or completely give up saying: *"This person is like this, this does not suit me, my presence at this meeting does not allow me to be myself..."*

We understand that this person's true god is within him and will lead him to give up his commitment under various pretexts. If the way another person acts, dresses or talks does not suit him, he prefers to withdraw.

Our analysis of others merely reflects our shortcomings, deficiencies and emotions. Beyond our wants and aspirations, there is an emotional reality within us that we are not aware of, which determines the way we relate to others.

The work of the prophets is to teach us to manage our family relationship legacy and to transform it into a blessing by bringing opposites into harmony. This is necessary so that our true Being, as conceived by divine love, can find his real identity. The process of transforming this relationship legacy into its opposite, i.e. from bad to good, allows our true Being to emerge, in accordance with the teachings of all religions.

This begins by ceasing to judge, that is ceasing to analyse others, and starting work upon the self. This consists in becoming aware of the presence of the 12 vices (arrogance, shame, pride, judgement, ostentation, jealousy, spite, complaining and so on) within us.

The work upon oneself consists of becoming conscious of the way these vices manifest themselves in us. To be aware of anger for example, we have to know what the signs of anger are and slowly, we reach the point when we are no longer dominated by anger. The same goes for shame, pride and the other vices....

Identifying these vices in our daily actions and working on them enables us to be aware of pairs of opposites within us. The transformation of something into its opposite can only happen within us, in our inner being. If we are to act in imitation of the prophets, we need to carry out this work on our family relationship legacy to attain the opposite of the 12 vices within us.

The content of this book is drawn from the writings of Sheikh Ahmadou Bamba. Let us take as illustration one of the examples that he gives, impatience. He says:

"It is the inability to wait for something or restrain oneself, the lack of patience, the inability to

bear someone or something. The impatient person is one who desires with anxious haste and who wants immediate results."

When we know the definition of impatience and are engaged upon our quest, we are attentive and remain watchful for signs of it to appear, in order not to be carried away. Otherwise, we are inflamed by reaction to such an extent that we do not take account of our pressing and anxious desire. We are not aware that we are unable to bear it and to understand the consequences of our impatience.

What are these consequences?

Sheikh Ahmadou Bamba enumerates them: *"Deprivation, discouragement, regret, disobedience, doubt, the wish to give up action in which one was engaged - the inability to 'hold out' as they say - and we find ourselves in a state of deprivation, discouragement, regret and disobedience."*

The awakening of consciousness will enable us to understand that impatience is accompanied by anger, feverishness, nervousness and questioning of orders issued ….

This often goes as far as making us say: *"I absolutely need this because mine is a special case"*. Hence certain people use dishonest and fraudulent means such as cheating to obtain what they want. All this relates to impatience but we are not aware of it.

Ceasing to judge others means we can now undertake work on ourselves. It is necessary to know how our impatience is manifested and to see what failings it arouses. Understanding the consequences of our actions not only enables us to stop analysing others but also to understand how the principle of action and reaction works in us.

There is not merely impatience but also the 11 other vices to identify in us, all born from our relationship legacy. Once we have identified them, we have to resolve the pairs of opposites within us - that is to transform our family relationship legacy, characterised by blame, conflict and rejection, into its opposite.

We will hence find our original Being as defined by various faiths, that is, the Being liberated from the yoke of the 12 vices. This personal and inner work enables us to rid ourselves of vices and to allow good will to descend from our heads to our hearts. Thus we become true Beings according to the teachings of various religions.

The being and religion

The message of Moses was that people must be liberated. How should we understand this? We must understand that this liberation concerns us and awakens the Jewish being within us. It is only by reconnecting with our condition as human beings that we can achieve liberation. For the followers of Jesus, this liberation means awakening the Evangelical being, just as for those who follow Islam, it means awakening the Qur'anic being.

Do you know of any prophet who asked people to which religion they belonged before working with them? None! The most important thing in their eyes was the human being and not any form of religion.

The attitude of Christ in the story of the woman taken in adultery is interesting in relation to this. The religious people of the Temple said:

"We shall go and see Christ with this prostitute to see what he will say in this situation."

They were calling upon religion. If Jesus condemned the woman, he was applying Moses' law but he would be contradicting himself as he preached compassion. If he applied his so-called religion, he would be going against

Moses. But he had said that he had not come to destroy the law but to fulfil it.

The people of the Temple said to him:

"This woman has committed adultery; what does religion say?"

We can see clearly that they were analysing the other person! Jesus answer directed them back to themselves:

"Let he who is without sin cast the first stone."

They had come to him as a religious man but he, considering only the human being, refocused their attention back on themselves, so that they could review their own condition.

What matters to God above all is the human being. When we understand the human being, we understand God's message. At that moment, we establish a relationship of true love with the divine for the human being is the reflection of God on earth. One cannot establish a relationship with God apart from through a relationship with human beings. We must not forget that the first human being was God Himself who decided to create man as his representative on earth.

The meaning we have given to religion does

not take account of all this. It has nothing to do with the truth. Instead, the message of God primarily takes account of the human being, and if one wants to be a Being of Peace, one must first of all take account of difference as a basic necessity of life.

The Lord Himself says:

"If He had wanted, He would have made of you only one community"

Qur'an C5 V48.

But He Himself was the first to create differences. And He asks us to respect *these differences and to excel through the capacities that He has given to each one of us, which differ from one person to another.*

So we see that through the divine message:

- We return to the human being who is at the beginning and end of all action.
- We return to the human being who is the centre of divine reality.
- We return to the human being who is the remedy for other human beings.

This is the essence of the divine message.
"The human being as seen by different religions" is only one Being - **he who understands that God's religion is above all the religion of the human being.** His work consists in bringing

the opposites within us into harmony, as the prophets did. This involves the ability to emerge from our blood family who has educated and conditioned us in order to belong to the global family.

To belong to the global family it is not enough to say "I belong to the global family" but one has **TO BE.** This consists in transforming our family relationship legacy in its opposite. The sum of all these opposites takes us back to love.

And then one goes back to the beginning of Creation - that is life which is an act of love. We do not have to give a meaning to life for the minute the harmony of opposites is achieved within us, we represent divine love on Earth. From the moment we establish our relationship with the Lord according to the rank He has given us, that of Servant, we are able to fulfil the Qur'anic truth:

"Man is the representative of God on Earth".

This is why Martin Luther King said:

"You don't have to know Einstein's theory of relativity to serve. You don't have to know the second theory of thermodynamics in physics to serve. You only need a heart full of grace, a soul generated by love."

This is the very basis of the True Being.

All this process of transformation leads us to gradually leave the framework of the family relationship legacy to move into the global family because these virtues enable us to become a creator of solidarity and sharing.

It is this in-depth work which is required from all human beings because each one of us has a family relationship legacy that he keeps within him and that he needs to transform.

What is required of any individual is just **TO BE,** to bring and to unite his loving heart and his generous soul with existing souls and hearts. Thus a new, better and happier society will be born and the Golden Age will dawn. It will no longer exist as an imaginary utopia.

CHAPTER 5

FORGIVENESS OR THE SCIENCE OF DIFFERENCE

We have seen that the relationship between parents and children is based on illusory rights and duties. He who does not respect the laws violates the liberty of the other and must be punished. This is how the child turns into a judge who condemns his parents who have not respected his rights and those of the other spouse. He sincerely believes that he is not responsible.

We sometimes hear children expressing this lack of responsibility to their parents. They say:

"I never asked to be born. You are responsible. So assume your responsibility and provide me with

what I need."

Inourworldbuiltonopposites,weareconfronted by the "responsibility / no responsibility" pair of opposites. Once again, without these opposites, life would not exist - for example, we would be in a perpetual night or day, which would not be life! The principle of opposites is poetically expressed in the Qur'anic verse: "He wraps the night up in the day, and wraps the day up in the night." This creates life. This also helps us in understanding ourselves: we experience the principle of external opposites with others and we experience the principle of inner opposites within ourselves. The latter leads us to self-transformation through the suspension of judgement.

Experiencing inner opposites means transforming negative into positive. Our family relationship legacy causes us great suffering at first by making us suffer emotional voids. Through the work of self-transformation, we discover that this legacy is a gold mine which enables us to become the Being that all religions call us to be.

On this basis we can escape from the trap of words. When you advise someone to forgive, it is as if you were asking him to transform evil into good! He finds this very difficult for in his daily life, he has always seen evil being punished. Why and how should we try to transform it?

Forgiveness is difficult only when we are analysing the other person. This is why forgiving requires firstly a change of outlook. This change of perspective brings about the transformation of the Being within us. To be able to transform oneself is the privilege of Man: he is able to become someone else compared to what he was before. This capacity for transformation is indeed the eternal message of God in all religions.

When we have made use of this capacity to forgive, we become forgiveness and mercy ourselves for ever. Once this stage has been reached, we are in the process of action. This means that we can enable others to leave the servitude of their sufferings to help them to be in their turn what we have become.

We therefore understand that no-one attempted to harm us or wanted to refuse us love and tenderness. But our parents and close relations were themselves victims of their own history and were therefore subject to the relentless law of repetition and reproduction. They were prisoners of their sufferings, not living freely in the present but remaining trapped in their own childhood judgements. Having never ceased to judge, they remained suffering victims and in their turn spread their suffering, whatever form it might take. This is how we as victims unconsciously become tormenters.

But if we follow the way that leads to forgiveness, we can understand that in condemning these "tormenters" we condemn people who are unconscious of what they do and who are themselves experiencing deep and unbearable suffering. In other words, we are condemning innocent people! Then our compassion is awakened and we can go as far as to ask their forgiveness for having judged them and added to their sufferings…

All our wealth resides within us: the original faith that we mentioned in the first chapter and kindness, love, and compassion; they are the essential components of a peace which alone can lead to happiness. But they are shadowed by our ego, the characteristic product of our family relationship legacy. We are born human: our task is to work on ourselves in order **TO BE.**

From the moment we stop passing judgements

that are driven by the ego born from our relationship legacy, we re-focus on ourselves, and the inner work, the work on **BEING**, starts. Behind the gold mine of self-transformation, the power of forgiveness is hidden. It is the key that allows us to unlock the treasure within us.

When we are in a state of being, it will be possible for us to produce a type of **HAVING** which is beneficial to all. Such a **HAVING** is made up of all the virtues that our childhood experiences enabled us to acquire, such as patience, the capacity to give and love unconditionally, the consciousness of the Absolute to whom our prayers are addressed, and the awareness of beauty. All this is possible thanks to pairs of opposites: we lacked something, which enabled us to discover its opposite. This is how we are placed in a condition where we can help others reach this level of profound and unalterable peace.

Let us not deplore the existence of the ego. It is a necessity as it is through the ego's transformation that we can rediscover the Being that we are. Through its ability to separate and divide, the ego is the entity within us that is conscious of difference. As a result, the essential work of transforming the ego gives us access to the concept of unity. In this sense, the ego is an indispensable component in our development.

Let us not go and seek the Being elsewhere but in us! Let us not seek transformation elsewhere. The Vedic, Evangelic, Jewish, Qur'anic being we spoke about earlier is within us. This is why we can declare that each one of us is a benefactor to humanity. Indeed, Liberation Therapy is not really a therapy, for there is no patient. There is only an aspect of ourselves that we cannot manage as we should for we are ignorant of its laws.

At both individual and international level, we are unaware that:
- religious difference feeds the ego
- cultural difference feeds the ego
- economic difference feeds the ego.

These differences nourish our ego and if we pay attention, we easily see that all of humanity's problems have been and are related to the ego, whether we are talking about:
- the First World War
- the Second World War
- the Vietnam War
- the war in Iraq
- the war between Tutsis and Hutus, and so on.

Before going further, it is important to remember why we are not in a state of peace today. As we have seen in the preceding chapters, it is first of all important to be aware of our conditioning to become conscious of our Being. Our conditioning starts at birth, within our family, at school and in society in general.

When we arrive in the large human family, we see differences. They are present in all aspects of life: in languages, lifestyles, ways of worshipping, cultural expression, level of wealth, etc.

Everything is different from us and our customs and beliefs. And there is difference even among differences! How can we cope with these multiple realities? If we are still in a state of judgement, we meet these differences with our particular preferences. We say that this is better than that, this is beautiful, and that is ridiculous, primitive, or savage... In distinguishing between differences, we dig chasms and establish deep divisions …

If we agree to go to the bottom of things, we see that in order not to be in a state of judgement, we need to learn how not to distinguish among differences and how to stop separating and dividing. This becomes possible only when we understand that difference is a necessity of life.

It is thanks to this difference that our life has a meaning. It allows us to be useful to one another and to be richer because of our complementing characteristics. Difference gives us more assets to understand the world surrounding us. To benefit from the unique advantages of this *science,* the *science of difference* and *forgiveness,* what must we do?

First of all, we must rediscover the first dark emotions of childhood. Then we need to accept them and accept ourselves through them - in other words, we have to accept our life in good faith, knowing that it is completely futile to dream of another life which has never and will never exist. The life that we are living is the one and only life that we could have, and it is also the best possible. Once we have accepted these emotions, we have access to them to transform them into their opposites.

What should we do to reach this point? Let us recall once more. Childhood experiences are an initiation to universal values. Adulthood is the maturation of these values. So, when we leave our close family we are perfectly conditioned to **HAVE** in order **TO DO** and **TO DO** in order

TO BE. This is tragically reflected in our absence of a true ideal: when love is absent, there is an absence of liberty and consequently an absence of choice.

To get out of this, we need to grasp our family, social, and historical relationship legacy and transform it in order to become a "Being" first and foremost. This Being will have the objective of **DOING** in order to **HAVE.**

Each one of us is in fact a benefactor to humanity if we manage our relationship legacy by transforming the low and exhausting energies of vices, not by suppressing them but by changing them into elevated, energy-giving virtues that bring peace and profound and contagious joy.

The objective is to live a balanced life - peace lies in the middle way. Divine inspiration has taught that the best community is one that practises the middle way. This is why each of us must make use of the subtle principle of opposites, the basis of creation and of our existence. The transition from one to the other is not achieved through suppression or control but by the transformation of one into the other (as shown by the teaching illustrated by the table on page 18). We must therefore endeavour to leave emotions behind, emerge from what we judge as evil, and transform it into its opposite. Such is the beginning of change.

Firstly, we have to give up all our preconceived ideas of people and events and begin to build an ideal, that is, we must start by giving up all the judgement that inspired our illusory ideal.

To achieve this development, we have to grasp the significance of:

- the necessity of the experience undergone, and
- the impact of this experience on the formation of our Being.

If we want to realise the ideal inspired by the married life of our parents, judgement renders the formation of our Being impossible.

Everyone agrees that the consequences of judgement are harmful. Everyone agrees we should condemn and prohibit judgement. But to reach the point of non-judgement, it is necessary for consciousness to be awakened.

We have to emerge from judgement and opinion for until now, our life has been affected by the opinion that others might have of us and that we take as a judgement. Opinion is not judgement; opinion does not assess the "do-er" but their deeds - it does not differentiate between the individuals involved. Everyone can and must give his opinion without setting himself up as a judge.

In our everyday life, we worry a lot about the opinion of others regarding who we are and what we do. This attitude takes us back to our childhood where our happiness depended solely on what our parents thought of us and their satisfaction or disappointment in us.

As adults, before taking the decision to do something, we ask ourselves: "Will my family or my relatives approve?" We are inhabited by the desire to win the approval of others and before taking action, we review in our mind all our acquaintances to see who will be "for" and who "against".

We are deciding whether to take action and in our desire for approval, we want to avoid a reaction. This is not possible! In the same way as we fear lack of acceptance, this fear of reaction takes us back to our childhood when we expected Mum or Dad to solve our problems. If we want to avoid reaction, we take action in secret.

The principle of action and reaction is a physical law ever present in our relationships. But as it relates to feelings, subjectivity and moods, we find it difficult to be aware of its existence.

It is the work of transformation that will free us from this trap because we escape from the principle of opposites. This is because from the moment the transformation of the self starts, we cease to be able to oppose others even if they oppose us. We are no longer in a state of duality.

In his book *The Tenth Insight,* James Redfield quotes Rosemary Altea:

"There is no magic potion…that gives us wisdom. Only our experiences will teach us and then, only if we are truly willing to learn. We can read a million books whose words inspire us, will help to point us in a certain direction. But only the experience can give us true meaning to the written word."

If it is judgement which leads us to integrate vices within us, in order to move to the opposite of vices, we have to understand what the opposite of judgement is…

This brings us to the universal key of forgiveness. Our reproduction of our parents' lives in our own lives, the consequence of our **judgements,** can only come to an end through the practice of **forgiveness.**

Forgiveness is an essential stage on the path to spiritual elevation. Forgiveness enables us to stop being a victim by breaking the bond which ties us to the emotions of the past. Our anger, bitterness, desire for revenge and all the suffering that these entail, stop immediately. We are no longer under the illusion that the past is continuing into the present, and we are no longer compelled to a pattern of repetition which inevitably makes tormenters out of us in our turn.

Forgiveness is also what Jesus expressed in these words:

"I tell you in truth, whoever will not enter the Kingdom of God as a small child will not enter it." (Luke 18:17).

Forgiveness is the art of being a child who knows no resentment. The child loves regardless of the attitude of the other person. He gives unconditional love - not due to lack of memory, for he remembers his sorrow. The difference is that he takes no account of it in the relationship with the person who caused it!

It is not a question of forgetting, that would be a pity. Everything that happens to us makes up our experience, and, hopefully, it will be the foundation of the wisdom that makes it possible for us to bring compassionate help to others. We should not hope that our memory will forget an offence: this is not possible, or could be the alarming symptom of a degenerative disease. What matters is that our heart is not embittered and that it remains peaceful as if the incident never took place, even if the action that hurts us remains in our memory. Actions become like shadows, inert and detached from ourselves; we are not them and they are not us. They do not form part of our identity.

The story of the Prophet Joseph illustrates this well. When his brothers arrived in Egypt and became aware that the Grand Vizier in front of them was really their brother Joseph whom they had ill-treated in their childhood, they wanted to recall the past to justify themselves or to apologise but Joseph interrupted them and said: "Today is not the time to remember all that, today is the time to forgive."

For Joseph had seen the emanation of the divine through his brothers. He understood that this order came from a higher power that wanted to lead him to a destiny that he had not imagined.

His brothers had been the mere instruments of this power. Joseph never even regarded them as guilty.

Let us say it again: forgiveness is the art of rediscovering innocence.

The practice of forgiveness makes us humanity's true benefactors. We immediately stop projecting ourselves onto our children and using their lives to fulfil ourselves through them, that is, using them to attain the objectives that we could not achieve because we were also in the process of reproducing our parents.

As we have seen above, the vicious circle of *"I do not want to experience what my parents experienced"* is transformed into *"I do not want my children to experience what I have experienced"* which can also be, in the version of imitation by veneration, *"My parents did everything the way it should be done. Why? Because that is the way it should be!"*

Forgiving is the art of acceptance, not through resignation but **through compassion**. It is an awakening of consciousness that occurs once we start to see more clearly through the chaos of our lives and which enables us to understand that if we have been trapped in a system leading us to reproduce acts we condemned, those who offended against us were hardly more likely to escape from the system. At this moment, becoming aware of the real problem, we understand that there is no need to condemn them. They have not had the chance to achieve consciousness! We see that they have been trapped and we cannot help but be compassionate and forgiving. Indeed, how can we bear grudges against people who are totally unaware of what they are doing?

When we understand the process of unconscious repetition of the past, characteristic of all humans before consciousness awakens, we discover that there was never a father who did not do his duty or a mother who did not show an interest. We are overcome with compassion and forgiveness.

Hence, we transform our family relationship legacy. It is no longer burdened by our evil thoughts about our parents. We see that if we did not have something, it was not because mother or father did not want to give us what we wanted or needed. It was not that they did not love us!

We stop experiencing a feeling of want. We stop establishing relationships with everyone else designed to fill the emotional gaps that we experienced with our parents. At this moment, we cease to feel any lack. There are no relationship gaps to fill or repair. We understand that our life is the best possible. We can therefore give and not ask anything in return. This is love! We have transformed evil into good through the power of positive thought and so followed the example of the prophets.

Young people often leave the family home because of family conflicts. A girl or a boy looks for a partner whose values are opposite to those of his/her family. That brings about a break with their family. The young couple will live "apart" for some time. There will be attempts at reconciliation, which are unsuccessful more often than not until grandchildren are born. They will be the ones to recreate the bonds. Grandparents love their grandchildren because once more, they see themselves through the children of their children.

But the evil is still there, still not healed.

The power of forgiveness gives everyone the possibility to leave their family circle without being inspired by their family relationship legacy. It is by the power of forgiveness that all the vices born of judgement stop having an influence over us and dominating everything that we do.

We reach a level where we become conscious of our choice and our ideal. In this consciousness of our choice, we are able to establish relationships where we no longer seek to fulfil an emotional gap.

We can come back to our families at peace with ourselves and a source of peace for others – we can even resolve the problems found there. To sum up, we can say that we leave the family as a son and come back as a "prophet" – we become a reconciler who embodies love. At this stage, we do not speak empty words for we ourselves incarnate the truth of what we say. This is how our family environment is transformed.

We can therefore see how powerful is the forgiveness that all prophets have taught without exception. When we say, "Lord, forgive us as we forgive those who have sinned against us", we are echoing the words of Jesus, but we must not say it as Jesus' prayer but our own. Each one of us has been placed in a situation where we can utter these words and then live them as Christ did. Each of our lives has similarities with the lives of the prophets.

Forgiveness also allows us to awaken the conscience of the guilty. How? By the grace of the victim who must face the person who made him suffer and his tormenter's own original faith, kindness, compassion and love. The victim opens within himself a space for forgiveness. And due to the fact that the victim has undergone a metamorphosis from the state of a victim to an embodiment of virtues, he rediscovers and revives these virtues in the offender. At this moment, the former victim transcends duality and opposites because he does not set himself up as the opposite of his tormenter - instead, he enfolds the offence in forgiveness.

We will not change anything that displeases us, that we do not like, or that we blame on others if we do not start by changing our inner selves. Seeking within ourselves, mining the wealth of our inner gold mine, allows us to reach the core of our being, that, as we have seen, is made up of kindness, compassion, love and original faith. We are no longer restricted to our individual, separate selves but our being encompasses the whole universe. Let us listen to the song of mystics who experienced unconditional love, the reflection of divine love.

"Love came;
It became the blood overflowing in my veins and under my skin.
Love emptied me of myself and
filled me up with the Friend,
All the fragments of my existence
are invaded by the Friend,
Of me, nothing remains
except the name."

(Rumi)

This love made them capable of embracing all differences:

"My heart has become capable of every form: it is a pasture for gazelles and a convent for Christian monks, and a temple for idols and the pilgrim's Ka'bah, and the tables of the Torah and the book of the Qur'an.

I follow the religion of Love:
whatever way Love's camels take,
that is my religion and my faith."

(Ibn Arabi)

CHAPTER 6

THE FORGIVENESS OF BEINGS OF PEACE

We can at this stage turn towards the great wise men, the prophets, the Beings of Peace, to examine how they put forgiveness into practice.

They endured much because of their actions, but in return they always showed love. They did not define themselves based on how others treated them. No, they were "different."

They had understood that forgiveness enables feelings of distress or hatred to be exchanged for positive and generous emotions. Through this exchange, the forgiver, as we have seen, has not merely liberated himself from his state of victimhood but places the offender in a situation where the latter can become happier. Gandhi used to say:

"The weak can never forgive. Forgiveness is the attribute of the strong. Abstinence [from punishment] is forgiveness only when there is power to punish; it is meaningless when it pretends to proceed from a helpless creature. Forgiveness is a quality of the soul and therefore a positive quality."

Many people, convinced of the importance of forgiveness, would like to practise it in their lives to free themselves from their past and find peace in their relationships with those close to them. But many do not know how to introduce it into their lives and how to attain the peace they desire.

In the wish to bring such people assistance, we have once again examined the lives of Beings of Peace who have marked history. We have chosen six among them, a little arbitrarily but also because of the diversity of their backgrounds and the ordeals they underwent. This analysis focuses on forgiveness as embodied by Sheikh Ahmadou Bamba, Gandhi, Martin Luther King, Nelson Mandela, Emir Abdel Kader and Captain Dreyfus.

We have hence learnt that there are four stages

in attaining the forgiveness that they practised so perfectly:

- De-conditioning

The three steps following de-conditioning are unconditional:

- Transformation of the desire for revenge into unconditional love
- Unconditional personal commitment
- Unconditional generosity of forgiveness.

Let us examine the content of these inner conditions for forgiveness.

1. De-conditioning

We saw in the first chapter that conditioning is the ground on which the 12 vices grow, polluting our soul and preventing it from achieving inner peace. De-conditioning is the break from the beliefs we have acquired from our history, family and culture that allows consciousness to awaken. This enables us to enter the reality of the present moment. De-conditioning is often the most important moment of one's life, a kind of shock where the individual finds himself in a situation where he questions his outlook on life generally and on his own life in particular. He is then able to reconsider the foundation of beliefs and habits. It is like a new birth that will propel him to a higher level of awareness.

Three of these Beings of Peace experienced this great initiatory moment during their childhood:

- Sheikh Ahmadou Bamba
- Martin Luther King
- Nelson Mandela.

Three others experienced it during adulthood:

- Emir Abdel Kader
- Gandhi
- Captain Dreyfus.

- Sheikh Ahmadou Bamba lost his mother at a very early age. This separation and the fact of being an orphan resulted in him becoming a completely de-conditioned Master. Indeed, instead of sinking into affliction, he was propelled at this tender age into a new universe, that of an awakened consciousness. He broke away from childhood for good. An exceptionally gifted child, a mystic poet at the age of eight, he was able to write long inspired prayers, highly poetical odes on manifestations of universal love. The major event which brought him to the attention of an astounded world was his refusal to succeed his father when as a young adult, he was invited to take over the important post of adviser to the king that his father held.

De-conditioning: In his emotional loss, he transcended filial love to focus it on the prophets, their companions and the divine Creator. He made himself the servant of the last of the prophets, the Prophet Muhammad, to whom he would devote his life and whose original message of peace and service to mankind he constantly strove to revive.

- Martin Luther King had a different experience as a child in the USA. As a son of a pastor, transcendence was familiar to him. He enjoyed the company of Terence, a white child who had always been his friend. But when he started school, he was propelled into a segregated world where his friendship with Terence became impossible. This separation from Terence plunged him into profound sorrow to which would be added all his parents' tales of tragedies and humiliations born of the racism of which blacks were victims. The child Martin was profoundly shocked.

De-conditioning: This series of painful events would give rise to unflagging efforts to achieve equality and unity between men of all races until his death.

- Nelson Mandela was born into a rich and

noble family in the second decade of the 20th century. His father was the "adviser and maker of kings." Following his father's refusal to obey the summons of a white magistrate ("I will not go, I am ready to fight") to answer an accusation of having allowed an ox to escape, the family's destiny took a turn for the worse. The Mandelas found themselves stripped of their aristocratic rank. They fell from being a royal family to being rural and common.

De-conditioning: The small Nelson derived from this experience a thirst for justice which he would always pursue.

- In the 19th century, an Indian lawyer was violently pushed from the train where he had dared to book a first class seat. His name was Gandhi. He spent that dark night of 4th April 1893 utterly alone on the platform of Maritzburg station in South Africa, confronted with humiliation and injustice. He would never refer to it except to say that it was the one of the most important moments of his life. The young lawyer saw all his hopes of social elevation ruined forever in spite of his studies and efforts until that point.

De-conditioning: The unknown lawyer would emerge from this night with a new energy and a different vision of the life he wanted for himself and all his brothers, whether they were Indians or British, white or brown, Hindus or Muslims.

- More astonishing is the fact that the awakening of Emir Abdel Kader followed a vision of Prophet Abraham who told him that from now on, he was to admonish believers. The message had such impact on him that it changed the course of the Emir's life forever.

De-conditioning: The Emir then perceived that there is another dimension to human relations. This warrior renounced all forms of violence.

- Lastly, a scandal in France at the beginning of the 20th century made Captain Dreyfus, a graduate from the elite École Polytechnique military school in Paris but also a Jew, the notorious hero of a miscarriage of justice caused by anti-Semitism. A soldier by vocation, he was betrayed by the French army in which he had put all his faith. The conspiracy affected him profoundly and irreversibly. All the values he believed in were shaken by this treachery. Victim of a plot woven by his superiors, publicly stripped of his rank, and exiled for five years to Devil's Island off Guyana, the ex-captain saw his whole world and external life collapse.

De-conditioning: Despite this shock, his desire for justice was so strong that he felt no anger nor made any claims throughout his ordeal.

2. Transformation of the desire for revenge into unconditional love

De-conditioning is usually a moment of great inner upheaval that generates enormous suffering. The injustice and suffering experienced bring about a revolution in consciousness. The loss of familiar reference points leads to an awakening. One emerges from the pattern of repetition and imitation and one is unwilling to inflict the same suffering on others. One is conscious that constantly hounding someone else is tantamount to sinking to the lowest level possible for a human being. The mature Being refuses to exist at this level of wrongdoing and to harbour a spirit of revenge for his own benefit. He understands that revenge brings neither reconciliation nor rehabilitation. Once he gives up revenge, he is able to experience unconditional love which will lead him to help both the oppressor and the oppressed.

One of the conditions of forgiveness is to remain neutral so as not to create division. The Being of Peace does not see himself as belonging to one group or another. He realises that dominators and dominated form a whole and that their relationship involves a pair of opposites that is indispensable to harmony. He no longer sees the person, the group or the ethnicity and so he does not condemn even if he denounces and opposes acts committed.

Gandhi is a significant example: in the violent conflict between Hindus and Muslims that raged in the troubled years following Indian independence, he called on people to transcend hatred. The British colonisers were taking advantage of the situation to "divide and rule" but he appealed to the Indians to avoid any kind of fanaticism and to practise tolerance and compromise.

Thus, he advised a Hindu demanding justice for the murder of his son by a Muslim not to nurture hatred in his heart but instead to bring up a Muslim orphan, removing all the hatred in his heart and forgiving those who had harmed him.

Sheikh Ahmadou Bamba provides an equally significant example of the transformation of the desire for revenge into unconditional love. When the French colonisers who feared his charisma condemned him to exile in Gabon, the Sufi Master only rejoiced and invited his disciples to follow him. Seeing only the manifestation of the divine in all things, he saw his sentence as an opportunity for spiritual elevation. He bore no hatred against those who inflicted this sentence on him - in his eyes, they were only instruments at the service of the divine. He said:

"May God give repentance and reconciliation to those who have insulted and blamed me" and "I have forgiven all my enemies with a pure and sincere heart."

Two men fought in different places against the same kind of apartheid - Nelson Mandela and Martin Luther King. They were also able to transform their anger into unconditional love during their ordeals.

When Nelson Mandela came out of prison and everyone expected him to call for a riot, eagerly awaited by the blacks and feared by the whites, he made a speech calling all to harmony. It was a speech full of compassion for those involved in apartheid and for the future of the country. As for Martin Luther King, we only have to consider his own words which sum up this stage perfectly:

"Love is not this sentimental something that we talk about. It's not merely an emotional something. Love is creative, understanding goodwill for all men. It is the refusal to defeat any individual. When you rise to the level of love, of its great beauty and power, you seek only to defeat evil systems. Individuals who happen to be caught up in that system, you love, but you seek to defeat the system."

Emir Abdel Kader illustrates the ability to go beyond any impulse for revenge, particularly in his great respect for prisoners of war. While prisoners were usually massacred by the victors, he set them free if he knew that he would not be able to meet their basic human needs. He twice carried out exchange of prisoners with Monseigneur Dupuch, Bishop of Algiers. It was the same universal compassion which inspired him to answer a letter of Mgr Dupuch, who asked him to spare the life of a French nobleman:

"I have received your letter. It did not surprise me after what I have heard about your holy nature…

However, allow me to tell you that in your double capacity as servant of God and friend of men, your brothers, you should have asked me not only for the liberty of one but of all the Christians made prisoner since the resumption of hostilities.

Moreover, would you not be twice as worthy of the mission you speak of if you did not satisfy yourself merely by procuring such a benefit for 200 or 300 Christians but extended the same favour to a corresponding number of Muslims languishing in your prisons. It is written 'Do to others what you would have others do to you.'"

There is another series of correspondence that reveals the state of mind of the author, Dreyfus, addressed to his wife, Lucie (*Lettres d'un innocent,* published by Fayard). This exchange was his only means of surviving imprisonment. His captivity on Devil's Island was extremely harsh. He was forbidden to walk around the island and his legs were chained at night. For almost five years, until his return to France on 1st July 1899, before and throughout his banishment to Devil's Island, husband and wife exchanged numerous letters in which Dreyfus expressed his sufferings and called for justice but never for revenge. These letters can be seen as his "moral will" as he says:

"Besides, as I have told you already, my long letters are too clearly the equally intimate and heartfelt expression of my sentiments and of my immutable will for it to be necessary for me to return to them. They are my moral will and testament.

Therefore, my dear Lucie, for your own sake, for us all, you must always do your duty, be resolved to gain your right – the right of justice and of truth – until the full light shines out; until all France is convinced – and she must be – whether I should live or die; for, like Banquo's ghost, I should come out of my tomb to cry to you all with all my soul, always and again, 'Courage, courage!' to remind my country, who thus tortures me, who sacrifices me – I dare to say it, for no human brain could resist so long such an appalling situation, and it is only by a miracle that I have been able to resist until now – to remind my country that she has a duty to fulfill, and that that duty is to throw a refulgent light upon this sad tragedy, to repair this frightful error that has endured for so long."

3. Unconditional personal commitment

The Being of Peace who practises forgiveness is above all a man alone. Not only must he face the conditions that those who fight him subject him to, but he must also face frustration and incomprehension from those who say they are on his side and suffer together with him (but not like him) and who await, throughout the persecution and suffering, for his call to retaliate.

All of us know about Nelson Mandela who preached national reconciliation. Many of his followers were astounded by his attitude, they had waited for revenge for so long. And now their leader came out of prison with quite a different plan. Indeed we can recall Mandela asserting with great determination:

"I have fought against white domination, and I have fought against black domination. I have cherished the ideal of a democratic and free society in which all persons live together in harmony and with equal opportunities. It is an ideal which I hope to live for and to achieve. But if needs be, it is an ideal for which I am prepared to die."

What is less known is his personal commitment to fight a scourge that rages in Africa and throughout the world: AIDS, the modern plague. At a time when numerous eminent people and politicians saw members of their family dying of AIDS and hid this out of shame, on 6th January 2005, Mandela publicly announced the death of his son from the disease. He thus showed that no human being should be condemned or rejected. He overcame his own suffering and offered it to the people, offering up his very self to make us stop condemning the unfortunate victims of the disease, who die alone and isolated.

Two other men, one in India and one in Africa, underwent imprisonment and suffering and took a similar stance to Mandela. They showed that personal and unconditional commitment, even if we displease the great majority by our attitude, is an unavoidable step in the forgiveness process.

In India, Gandhi exposed himself to the physical violence of repression and imprisonment as part of his campaign of civil disobedience. He led a life of poverty and extreme asceticism, kept fasts that could have been fatal (paying no attention to his health even when he was growing old) and was determined not to stop as long as violence lasted and as long as his words and ideas remained ineffective against the waves of violence among ethnic groups caused by cultural and religious differences.

In Africa, Sheikh Ahmadou Bamba was deprived of his liberty for 33 years, sent from prison to prison and from exile to house arrest, but he never stopped pursuing his ideal of love and benevolence for the whole of humanity.

He accepted every humiliation without anger and never gave up his plan to create a better model of society, to be established not only for the welfare of his people alone but for all, white and black, friend and foe, friend and stranger, in his time and in the future.

As for Martin Luther King, he dedicated his short life to preaching the truth, no matter what it would cost him, whether he was understood and supported or not. Let us listen to what he himself asserted:

"And during the early days of my ministry, I read the Apostle Paul saying, *'Be ye not conformed to this world, but be ye transformed by the renewing of minds.'* I decided then that I was going to tell the truth as God revealed it to me. No matter how many people disagreed with me, I decided that I was going to tell the truth."

In 1860, a bloodbath in Damascus resulted from the conflict between the Druze and the Christians. Emir Abdel Kader, moved by compassion in the face of such suffering and in spite of his betrayals by the Christian West, risked his own life to save millions of Christians whose lives were in peril from the Druze revolt. Accompanied by 300 Algerians and two of his sons, he travelled across the district where the riot was raging, shouting:

"O Christians, O unfortunate ones, listen, come to me. I am Emir Abdel Kader, son of Muhiyyuddin, the one from Maghreb. Have faith in me. I will protect you."

Eventually, when the situation became calmer, he proclaimed that he would pay 50 dollars for each Christian brought to him. He thus saved more than 12,000 Christians.

Years later on Devil's Island, Dreyfus continued his correspondence with his wife. Innocent victim of a miscarriage of justice which turned out to be a conspiracy against him, he had no hatred in his heart for the people who deceived him. He understood the anger which drove these simple and credulous people and could even detect in their shouts an honour whose qualities he could not help but recognise. He confided in Lucie:

"I do not want to speak of my journey, it would break your heart. Know only that I have heard the legitimate cries of a brave and generous people against him whom they believe to be a traitor, the lowest of wretches."

4. Unconditional bounty

The Being of Peace does not take advantage of his attitude for his personal benefit. Whether he accepts or refuses distinctions or the Nobel Prize for his actions, it is never for himself as personal fame was never his goal. But this is often the way that his opponents deftly switch from opposing him to showing their gratefulness or admiration.

Inspite of his fame, success, personal renown and action in the world, Gandhi never modified his internal or external way of life. At the crowning moment of his assassination, a moment of ultimate solitude, Gandhi uttered words of forgiveness for his murderer. He had no other motive than respecting his commitment, no other motivation than being true to himself. Up to his last breath, he believed profoundly that it was his duty to testify to the astounded world his faith in nonviolence and his desire to love and serve humanity.

One day, an Arab agent of the colonisers tried to kill Sheikh Ahmadou Bamba. He was prevented and the Sheikh's disciples were about to kill him, but the Sheikh stopped them and told the man to flee. The man returned several times and was saved by the Sheikh who would say to his disciples:

"Let him go. Wouldn't you be happy if God forgave you?"

And he would ask the man to leave but not without having given him a gift. One day, the same man came to visit him at Diourbel. The Sheikh defended him once more, saying jokingly:

"Ah, it is the man who has lost his senses again!"

Then he sent him away, not without having given him a gift.

While he was under house arrest, the Sheikh gave money to the French who wanted to build a dispensary. He also made a donation of 500,000 francs in France to sustain the franc when it was threatened with devaluation, which would have destabilised the local economy. The Sheikh contributed one twelfth of the total of 600,000 francs that was collected in Senegal.

Finally, due to his exceptional behaviour, France decided to award him the title of Knight of the Legion of Honour which was the most honourable and coveted distinction that France could award. But Sheikh Ahmadou Bamba gently declined this offer, explaining that as he had acted only in faithfulness to his beliefs, he wanted no recognition or remuneration except from his Creator.

Once he had achieved victory and the work of the Truth and Reconciliation Commission had started, Nelson Mandela was elected President of South Africa. But he kept this position only while he was setting up structures for change. As President, Mandela was more of a head of state than a head of government. He assigned this role to Thabo Mbeki. As he had promised at the time of his election, Mandela did not stand for a second term and left politics. He never struggled for the sake of power - he worked for a cause greater than himself, and he acted as a kind of conscience for his country during its reconstruction. In 1999, Thabo Mbeki succeeded him as President.

Scarcely a few years earlier, Martin Luther King chose to wage a truly dangerous struggle in complete awareness of what he was doing. What mattered to him above all was the purity of his actions and total liberty with regard to any kind of recognition from the world. At the times when he faced fierce opposition and was under perpetual threat, he showed the foresight of a visionary. The following extract shows that he never attached the least importance to recognition from others. All his interest was focused only on the human being for whose sake he applied all his energies and took every risk:

"If any of you are around when I have to meet my day, I don't want a long funeral. And if you get somebody to deliver the eulogy, tell them not to talk too long. Every now and then I wonder what I want them to say. Tell them not to mention that I have a Nobel Peace Prize, that isn't important. Tell them not to mention that I have three or four hundred other awards, that's not important. Tell him not to mention where I went to school.

I'd like somebody to mention that day, that Martin Luther King, Jr., tried to give his life serving others. I'd like for somebody to say that day, that Martin Luther King, Jr., tried to love somebody. I want you to say that day, that I tried to be right on the war question. I want you to be able to say that day that I did try to feed the hungry. I want you to be able to say that day that I did try in my life to clothe those who were naked. I want you to say, on that day, that I did try, in my life, to visit those who were in prison. I want you to say that I tried to love and serve humanity."

Deeply mystical, his heart and soul purified

by the practice of ascetic piety that was never stained by any praise, decoration or honour, Emir Abdel Kader was only concerned with reconciliation between Muslims and Christians, expecting nothing in return. He wrote in a philosophical book that he sent to the Société Asiatique in Paris in 1885: "If Muslims and Christians would listen to me, I would put an end to their conflicts, they would become brothers both externally and in their inner hearts." He had no ulterior motive and sincerely wished for the happiness of all, friend or foe, uniting them in the same compassion and only seeing in each a human being loved by God.

As for Dreyfus, we will refer to Jacques Chirac's declaration when he was President of the French Republic:

"Let us not ever forget that the man who was rehabilitated to shouts of 'Long live Dreyfus!' answered with a strong voice:
'No! Long live France!' In spite of his humiliation, his exile, his sufferings, wounded in his heart and in his flesh, harmed in his dignity,
Captain Dreyfus was able to forgive.
Magnificent forgiveness, magnificent answer: love of country against intolerance and hate."

The rehabilitated Dreyfus served his motherland

again to the best of his ability during the First World War. This stoic never appealed to pity but only sought justice. His letters (mentioned above) inspired Zola, who raised public awareness of the Dreyfus affair, to say:

"I do not know of any pages of a higher conception or more eloquent. They have attained the sublime in sorrow, and afterward will endure like an imperishable monument when our own writings perhaps shall have passed into oblivion."

Inspired by such eminent examples, we can also attempt to follow the path of liberating forgiveness. We can put into practice Sheikh Ahmadou Bamba's advice to those who were ill treated or persecuted in various ways. This advice is like a key which can help us escape from victimhood. He said in *Masalik-Al-Jinaan – Itineraries to Paradise*:

"Bear them no resentment
When they are unjust,
When they refuse you a service or a favour,
When they harm you.
Be aware that they are under the power of the Lord
who holds them in His authority at all times…
Avoid harming them,
Recognise their rights,
Be patient,

Show magnanimity in the face of the harm
that comes from them.
Always practise towards them this policy
of wisdom and just words of mercy without
any kind of jealousy. Perfect your character,
Treat them gently while you turn yourself towards
God in your inner self. Be soft and kind to all,
Purify your heart,
Love for them what you love for yourself.
Be worthy of trust. Turn to the Lord when
faced with their injustice for this is a substitute
for worship..."

As Gandhi said, forgiveness is a quality of the soul. We have role models – those who want what they wanted have but to follow them!

CHAPTER 7

REAL LIFE STORIES

To return to daily life, here are some examples of the awakening of consciousness in some people whose life stories may be similar to ours. These people were living more or less tolerable lives, or perhaps less tolerable, like many of us. However, in a certain respect this was an opportunity for them since it allowed them to see their lives in a different light.

They took a path back to their childhood in order to identify what had taken control of their lives in their place. There they found a father who, through their eyes as a child, had been overly authoritative or a mother who was insufficiently protective. They became aware of how they had judged and condemned these parents and how they had been led to live the same story with a different partner.

This realisation gave them the clues necessary to free themselves from their past and work to attain the state of liberating forgiveness. Some are still on the way, but others have already achieved success, thanks to their efforts. For understanding is only a part of the process. We then need to use the light of awareness to illuminate the dark shadows that still exist in the present, poisoning our relationships.

In order to understand what can produce the emotions experienced in childhood in our adult life, we have chosen to provide some significant examples. The people mentioned here have of course given their consent so that their life story, whose traps they have been able to evade thanks to Liberation Therapy, can help others. We thank them in assisting those who will follow this path, which has enabled them to understand their inner self and return to their true Being.

First we are going to tell Fawzia's story, which shows how judgement starts the process of unconscious repetition of what we condemned in childhood. This process leads us irrevocably to re-live what we have tried desperately to escape. We invite those who can find similarities with their own lives to deepen their knowledge of Liberation Therapy.

Fawzia's story

Fawzia was born into a Muslim family of 11 children. Islam was taught as a religion of authority in their house. Her father was very authoritative and strict with the children, and jealous and suspicious of his wife. Fawzia's mother was naturally gentle and calm. She had got married very young, and immediately found herself under the yoke of her husband who never gave her either the chance or the right to take any decisions. Fawzia's father also made all of the financial decisions as he was the sole breadwinner.

Half of the children found the father too strict without, however, hating him. Even though the younger ones had a more positive opinion of him, everyone agreed that their mother had suffered too much and for too long.

Fawzia was never close to her dictatorial father. He frightened her and she did not feel loved by him. She felt closer to her mother, whom she saw as a victim of masculine domination. She perceived an inferiority complex in her mother that resulted from being a woman in a Muslim household.

Although she never talked about it and was not even aware of her thoughts, Fawzia nonetheless judged and condemned her father. This state of affairs nurtured within her contempt for Muslim men in general.

Despite his character, Fawzia's father was quite open-minded for his time since he was willing to let his daughter leave the family home to study abroad. Fawzia took the opportunity, and went to Europe. And it was there that she met her first suitor. As she was convinced that marriage to a Muslim man of the same nationality would mean that she would endure the same fate as her mother, she chose a British man of another religion as her husband.

However, though he is European and a non-Muslim, her husband has some of her father's character traits: he is authoritative, jealous, always has the last word and takes the final decision in everything. Unconsciously dominated by her condemnation of her father, Fawzia has reproduced her family background. With time, she has realised that her husband is just like her father and that she has ended up with practically the same fate as her mother but in a different country and environment.

Just like her mother, she experiences fear that makes her bend unflinchingly to her husband's decisions and that crushes her personality.

Fawzia continues to live in this situation as she has not yet forgiven her father, and she still hates anything to do with Muslims. Of course, she does not practise Islam, but she has adopted a different culture without converting to another religion. Marrying a European and living in Europe have not freed her as she had imagined. On the contrary, she cruelly lacks liberty of action, liberty of choice, and liberty to take decisions and to put her ideas forward.

Mark's story

Mark is a young man who got married to Nathalie five years ago. He has a good reputation at work, a young daughter and everything to make him happy. However, the couple faces serious problems. They finally asked for help from one of our therapists.

Mark's childhood was not a happy one. His father was an irritable man and when he came back from work, there were arguments that often degenerated into insults and blows, borne principally by Mark's mother. Mark suffered from this greatly and wanted to protect her. But it made him bitter that when his father fought him, his mother never intervened and left him to face the fear and threats alone.

Deeply traumatised by his terrifying father, Mark left the family home at a young age. He could no longer bear the tense atmosphere and more than anything else, he wanted to escape from the violence of the father whom he hated.

When he met Nathalie, he was thrilled. She had had a childhood just like his and understood him very well. Fear had also been her faithful companion. However, she was less bitter than Mark as her mother always sided with her in difficult times. She had been able to experience her mother's love and compassion and to feel protected.

Mark and Nathalie therefore decided to get married. Mark was impatient to live the ideal life that he had always dreamt of and which would certainly be different from the one that he had experienced with his father. Nathalie for her part shared this dream and thought it would come true.

It took the couple only a few weeks to become disillusioned. After a few arguments, Mark slapped Nathalie for the first time. Then he slapped her on countless occasions. When Mark saw that his wife was on the point of leaving, in a sudden moment of clear-sightedness, he suggested that they see our therapists as a last resort.

After a few appointments, Mark understood. He had closed the door on his past but it had never left him. He had condemned his father and left. He thought the whole business was over. However, in his distribution of roles he had attributed that of victim to himself and had retained it. There was no doubt that he had left, but what he was running away from remained profoundly rooted in him. The role of victim linked him closely to his past, and it was this past that ruled his life. Mark did not live in the present: he was a bystander in his own life.

And Nathalie had also played her part in their relationship breakdown. She had found in Mark a young man who told her what she wanted to hear:

"You know, I've suffered so much from what happened with my father… I don't want to live the same way any more… with you it will be different: love and tenderness…"

These words resonated with her as they had for him and they raised the same hopes. Nathalie and Mark thought they were identical, "soul mates". They felt that they were experiencing great love and that they were made for each other. Nathalie did not want to relive her traumatic past either, but she was dominated by it in spite of herself.

Nathalie had conceived a great admiration for her mother, whom she saw as a perfect model. When she unfortunately found herself confronting a violent husband, she followed her family example and played her mother's role, protecting her children at all costs. She had unconsciously given herself a way to embody what she had admired in her mother by marrying Mark.

Once their consciousness had been awakened, they had to find new reference points and be careful to "act", and not "react" blinded by their past. Their awakened consciousness allowed them to discover who they really were and what they really wanted.

Indira's story

In India, Indira hated men because of the relationship between her father and mother, and from which she suffered. Her father didn't care for his wife and the girl conceived a terrible grudge against her father. She became a firm feminist and was greatly interested in the situation of women. No matter what the issue under discussion, she would always ask sooner or later: "And what about women?"

As a young girl, she felt constantly neglected. She therefore worked hard to achieve a good social status and the approval of her peers. Then she got married. She met Prince Charming - but he was only charming while they were engaged. Once married, she realised that her husband reminded her of her father.

After some time, the couple had a son. Thinking of giving him the best education, Indira did everything possible for him and gave him everything that she herself would have liked as a child. As she did this, she did not realise to what extent she was stealing her son's life from him in order to repair her own.

Faced with the chaos in her life, Indira took the decision to try and use Liberation Therapy. Her successful awakening of consciousness allowed her to pull herself together and to make the necessary changes within her to break this reproductive cycle, to rediscover her husband, and give her son the chance to develop based on his own choices.

Claire's story

Claire was shocked when her father informed her that he wanted to get married after his divorce. It was not this announcement itself that shocked her, but the fact that her father had chosen a young woman of her age as his spouse.

Claire judged and settled the matter by roundly condemning her father and his young wife. As revenge, she was as hateful and unbearable as she could be to the couple and, with her brothers and sisters as her army, she waged a masterly war against her young step-mother. Then Claire left the family home, filled with all the judgement linked to her family history, and got married to the man of her life.

Of course, the man of her life was approximately the same age as her father! And she inevitably found herself at home with the children of his first marriage who quickly made her experience the suffering which she had inflicted on her father's wife! Once again, Liberation Therapy and forgiveness helped her to get rid of this "fate".

These cases are numerous. We can say without exaggeration that 80% of men and women find themselves trapped in this cycle of reproducing the family relationship model. The next story is another example.

Jean-Pierre's story

When Jean-Pierre came to see us one evening, he was tormented and worried: he realised that he was losing the ones whom he loved because of his uncontrollable violence. His wife had told him that she wanted to leave and she would not let him see his children.

We asked him to relate what he remembered from childhood.

"When I was a child, Father was violent to Mother for no reason. One evening he even broke two of her ribs. I could not bear to see my mother suffer. One day, I climbed on my father's back to prevent him from beating her. I was the only one among the six of us to show my father what I thought of his violence. He beat us with his belt to discipline us..."

We then asked him to tell us what was happening now at home with his wife and children. Jean-Pierre sadly replied:

"I beat my wife whenever she doesn't agree with me or whenever she answers back. I beat her several times even when she was pregnant. I even injured

her. It's true that I shout because I'm sure I'm right. I always need to be right. When I hit her, I know I'm not right. I take the belt to the children as well and beat them until blood comes to discipline them..."

Jean-Pierre had condemned his father and was at the same time on his mother's side. He had always idealised her. He was the only child to express disapproval of his father's violence. It was this attitude and judgement that cropped up when he became an adult. He therefore married a woman just like his mother. And confronted with his wife who embodies his mother, he has developed his father's character and become just like him.

Jean-Pierre has clearly understood the mechanism that imprisoned him in his own history. We don't know at the moment if he has won his wife's trust again, but we are sure that he now has the means to escape from his fate, thanks to his awakening of consciousness which allowed him to stop repeating his own painful childhood on others.

Marina's story

Marina was in her mid-forties and had a strong character: we could say that she was dominating. She was going through a difficult time: she could not control her anger, frequently directed against her husband. Worried and tense, she asked us to help her. We learnt that as a young girl, she was very fond of her father, who had a normal relationship with her mother. Unfortunately her father died, and her mother remarried. This time, the couple did not have any children.

The second husband was seen as very harsh by the children of the first marriage, and Marina had a difficult life. Moreover, her mother remained very passive. In spite of traumatic moments for her children, she never defended them and left them to their step-father's violence.

Marina used this situation as a basis to shape her ideal of a man. She did not take long to meet someone who was perfect for her. It was true love, of course, followed by a big wedding.

She told us, with some emotion in her voice:

"I lost my father when I was a child. My mother got married soon after. Her new husband was harsh with us. Mother let him do as he wished and she was often angry, especially with us kids. She used vulgar words.

"She said that I was jealous of my step-sister; she

told me that I was not worth anything. She often beat me a lot. I did all the household chores but she was never happy… she never defended me against my step-father.

"I left home very early. When I was sixteen, I got married. I thought I had found the ideal husband, the complete opposite of my step-father. But not long after, he started to beat me too.

"When I was 30, we got divorced and I remarried two years later. And then, I don't know what happened! It is as if an inner violence has built up in me. I can throw crockery or anything within reach at my husband's face. I hit him. I insult him and use terrible words…"

What we must understand from this situation is: as a child, Marina had condemned her mother and her second husband. At first, she married a man who reproduced the same behaviour as her violent mother. She pursued her role of a victimised girl in this relationship. Then, just like her mother after her husband's death, she married for a second time. She chose as a husband a man who would play the role of her passive mother when faced with her step-father's violence. Her husband would represent and embody Marina's mother, in a male body. Marina, dominated by her step-father's hateful memory, would embody him in the excess of violence which she condemned in him. She would be her step-father in a female body... During the couple's therapy, all these factors were considered. Both realised that they were not really living their own lives.

This shows us the importance of the soul in relation to the body. Emotions affect our mind, our soul and our heart. They have nothing to do with sex – the body is only a vehicle, it is inner feelings that matter.

Marina clearly understood, thanks to the Therapy, that she was reproducing exactly the family of her childhood. She instantly went to the extreme of suggesting divorce. We made her realise that divorce is not the ideal solution. Then she worked on her inner self to be able to apply the principle of forgiveness towards her parents. Little by little, she emerged from the role of victim that her judgements had made her play. The experience of forgiveness and the consequences of judgement made her decide to give up judgement for ever. This decision brought some peace between the couple.

Josephine's story

We were given the opportunity to meet a young man of 28, Jamal, who came to see us because of the breakdown of his relationship. He came with his wife Josephine; both were conscious that "something" was wrong: the true love, perfect companionship and intimacy that had led them to get married had disintegrated over time into violence and misunderstanding.

After five years of marriage, things were not going well. Jamal was from the South, an Egyptian. He was the fourth child of a family of eight: four girls and four boys. Jamal's religious education had made him a fundamentalist.

On the other side, Josephine, a young woman from the north of France, had in her childhood taken her father's side for in her eyes, it was her mother who "wore the trousers" and assumed the role of the husband. This made her want to give more authority to her father.

We can see how their family legacy brought them to see each other as ideal. Owing to his education, Jamal's ideal wife was a submissive woman, and due to her childhood, Josephine would look for an authoritative husband.

In fact, everything happened as if Josephine was trying to give her father the place that should have been his. This wish, born when she was 17, would be fulfilled at 22 when she met Jamal.

And to become his wife, according to both her and Jamal's way of thinking, she would have to embrace Islam and become a traditionally submissive woman, as her husband's culture demanded and in order for her husband's authority to be exercised. For Josephine, this marriage enabled her to restore her father to the role of husband.

Jamal had a fundamentalist father whom he had idealised. He wanted to reproduce this situation and so he looked for a woman as submissive as his mother.

The couple functioned on this basis for ten years, until the day when their relationship began to make the French woman feel suffocated. She soon realised that she was living her parents' life but with an unexpected subtle detail: the person whom the child has condemned can be played by a partner of another sex. In her case, her mother was represented by her husband whereas she embodied her father's submissive and self-effacing manner.

Then everything became clear. Josephine understood that her life had brought her to condemn her mother and to defend her father whom she perceived as a victim but whom she had at the same time taken as her ideal. As a reaction, she had therefore strived to embody her father. When doing this, she had not realised that to succeed, she needed somebody who would play the role of the mother. And her husband would play this role perfectly.

It was this that drove her to choose Jamal and that brought her to embrace the religion that went with this situation. In this particular case, by "religion" we mean a culture and not the experience of faith. She then found out that she had been truly living, but rather that she had dedicated her life to reproducing her parent's relationship.

Starting the therapy has enabled her to view things differently and to take the opposite approach. She has been able to re-experience the original feelings which had brought her to judge and to transform them into their opposite. The key to this change was in fact forgiveness, from where she was able to begin to take action strongly rooted in her mind.

This has enabled her to take up her life with her own identity. She would be Josephine, with her own ideal way of being.

Alain and Nadine's story

Nadine is a young and beautiful girl of 20

from Mali. Her father, the head of the family, presented himself as an exemplary believer, close to the fundamentalists and an influential figure of authority. Nadine as a child was the traumatised witness of the stormy relationship between her father and mother, based as usual on religion and culture.

This affected her so much that she was determined to marry a husband who would not be religious, and belonged neither to the same culture nor to the same race. She felt she was making a total break with her background. And one day, she met Alain, a European, her soul mate!

Unfortunately, soon all the similarities that Alain shared with Nadine's father appeared: a fundamentalist Christian, well-respected in his environment, with a strong religious education just like him, and who used the same language. Nadine found herself experiencing the same sequence of events that her mother had undergone.

For his part, Alain was enacting his own father's role. After using the Therapy's method, Alain and Nadine understood that they never were Alain and Nadine and that their relationship was only the embodiment of their parents' relationships. Their efforts focused on finding out who they really were, in order to at last be able to form their own relationship.

Dany's story

One of our therapists related the following experience:

"Dany was in his thirties when he met me 'to give weight to his life' (as he put it). The first time that I saw him, I thought him particularly thin, if not to say skinny. He always walks lightly and seems not to put any weight on the ground. Later I learned that he is a vegetarian and doesn't drink. It is useful to know that his mother is a Christian and his father a Hindu.

"Soon he told me about the big problem impeding his life: Dany is a homosexual, but with one detail: he has never acted on it. This is not because he refuses, but he has not found an opportunity. However, he has talked about his homosexuality to others and met with rejection.

"It is perhaps also owing to the double religious influence of his parents that Dany has always been on a sort of mystical quest that led him to spend four years in a Buddhist community in the centre of France. He worked there as a cook and experienced moments of happiness. Besides, he remembers with emotion and gratitude the person in charge of the temple to whom he confided that he was homosexual and who spontaneously replied: 'Well, at least, you love human beings!'

"I recall perfectly that at first sight, he gave me the impression of a lost soul, wandering without knowing which way to go. During our meetings, I realised how right this first impression was.

"Without being conscious of it, Dany does indeed personify indecision. He cannot commit himself and can see only the surface of things. He is a bit of a bystander in his own life, and his plans fail before they are born: one day he wants to go for training to get a job, the next day he plans to go to Great Britain as he speaks English well… But so far, he hasn't moved from where he was born. My impression was right: his physical appearance reveals his inability to take a decision.

"He explains his homosexuality by events that occurred in his life and form part of his bad memories: until the age of six, Dany slept between his father and mother. He could not sleep until his mother came to bed for he says 'she protected him.'

"On certain nights however, he heard noises that awakened and terrified him as he associated them with the violence to which his mother was subjected. Eyes closed, his heart pounding, he listened. He now says that these noises at night made something in him 'break'.

"To the adult Dany it seems that having relationships with women would mean acting like his father, something he does not want at any cost as he has condemned his father. So to avenge his mother, he has chosen to pay attention to men only.

"Dany's therapy is not complete, it has gone on and on. After having rented a small flat where he lived alone for some months, he has now returned to his parents' home. At this stage in his development, this return is positive in the sense that he is in a situation where he will be able once and for all to resolve all the conflicts of which he has now become fully conscious."

CASE STUDY: Mary and Bob (narrated by a therapist)

Here we witness a therapy session as if broadcast live, involving a couple on the point of breaking up. We have decided to present it to you to show how a person's feelings in the past rule his life without him being aware of it and how through expressing them, the person will become aware of this phenomenon and able to free himself.

Once he has cleared this up, he will be able to know what he truly wants and take the necessary steps to get it.

Here is the account given by one of the witnesses:

"We were having an informal meeting sitting in a nice garden, talking quietly as night was falling. A woman in her mid-forties was among us. It was Mary, whom we had met before. During the conversation, we asked her about her husband. Mary replied, somewhat uncomfortably, that everything was all right.

Sheikh Aly N'Daw asked her with a smile what was wrong. Mary replied that her private life could not be disclosed in public. Sheikh Aly reassured her that she was with her friends, this would do her good, and it would be useful to many of those who were there.

'So,' he resumed, 'How is Bob? He is my great friend. I care about him a lot, I saw him recently, and I'd like to see you back together!'

Mary started to cry. Her emotion was evident in the moonlight. Sheikh Aly quietly asked her to stop crying. She tried hard to wipe away her tears, and opened her heart bravely:

'Things are not going well between Bob and me. He spends his time playing football, or else he spends all day with his brothers. I have given my life to him, I have given up everything for him, my job, my family, the place where I was born… everything! And I've only received sadness in return. I now understand that he did not deserve so much sacrifice. Two months ago, it was the last straw. He forgot our wedding anniversary! I had prepared his favourite food that evening and I waited for him for hours. And finally he called me to tell me that he was going to spend the night at his eldest brother's place. After he hung up, I made up my mind; I packed my suitcase and left… I have not returned since. It's all over between us. I can no longer bear a man who only thinks about himself!'

After some time, Sheikh Aly asked, 'Has he tried to get in touch with you?'

'Yes,' replied Mary, 'many times. He has put on

an act as always. He cried, and told me that he loves me dearly. But this time it's over. I will no longer give way.'

Sheikh Aly: 'How long have you been together?'

Mary: 'Eleven years.'

Sheikh Aly: 'Eleven years! And those 11 years spent together will go up in smoke?'

Mary, angry: 'Bob needs to be taught a good lesson!'

'We all need lessons,' replied Sheikh Aly.

Mary: 'He has hurt me a lot!'

Sheikh Aly, smiling: 'You love him a lot!'

Mary was silent.

Sheikh Aly said: 'He loves you a lot as well.'

'No!' said Mary. 'I don't think that Bob loves me! In any case that's not how I see it at the moment.'

'Well,' said the Sheikh, 'when you went away,

he called you, so he still cares for you.'

Mary: 'He was putting on an act, as always!'

Sheikh Aly: 'Do you wish to live with Bob?'

Mary: 'Yes but…'

Sheikh Aly: 'Yes or no?'

Mary: 'Yes but…'

Sheikh Aly: 'Yes or no?'

Mary: 'Ye…y…yes…'

Sheikh Aly: 'Then you both want the same thing.'

Mary: 'I do. But I don't think he wants to.'

Sheikh Aly: 'You *think* so…but are you sure he doesn't want to?'

Mary, after a moment of silence: 'Even if he wants to, I don't want to any more after what he has done to me. It is no longer possible.'

Sheikh Aly, smiling: 'But you just replied yes to

the question about whether you wanted to live with him.'

Those present smiled in turn. Mary started to cry again.

Meg, a friend of Mary's, stood up and said: 'I know Bobby very well. Mary has tried everything. Bob doesn't know how to love. He is only interested in football and his brothers. He can spend all of his time doing these things now! He has made Mary suffer a lot, so it's now his turn to suffer. Bob doesn't deserve Mary's love!'

Sheikh Aly: 'Who are we to pass judgement on our brothers and sisters?'

Meg: 'Do you mean to say that Bob is right and that Mary is wrong?'

Sheikh Aly: 'Nobody is right, nobody is wrong. Judgement belongs only to God. In every prayer we say that He is the only judge but after prayer we take His place and start judging again!' (Those present laughed.)

Sheikh Aly, talking to Mary: 'Can you talk to me about your childhood?'

Mary: 'I don't recall my childhood.'

Sheikh Aly: 'What do you have against your parents?'

Mary: 'I loved them a lot.'

Sheikh Aly: 'God has placed a lot of love between parents and children! What do you have against them?'

Mary: 'Nothing. They gave me everything.'

Sheikh Aly: 'Can you talk about the relationship that you had with your parents?'

Mary: 'It was nice.'

Sheikh Aly: 'Yes, yes…And what else?'

Mary lowered her head. The silence was heavy.

Sheikh Aly: 'Our parents are our first spiritual masters. We have to thank them a lot for what they've done for us. How were your parents, Mary?'

Mary burst into tears: 'I pray for my parents but…'

Sheikh Aly: 'But?'

Mary: 'I have a grudge against them somehow. They didn't take time to take care of me. They worked all the time. Not only was I left to myself but on top of that, I had to take care of my brothers and sisters too.'

Sheikh Aly: 'We have to thank God that they didn't do anything for you. This has enabled you to be more independent. And to become an adult, we have to learn to rely on ourselves and trust God only. All the prophets had to rely on themselves in difficult times to bring God's message to light. If your parents had done anything for you, you would have been tied to them. After their death, you would have been in great confusion.

'There is an African proverb that says that when the parents die and the son cries bitterly it means that during their lifetime, the son was like a king. You cannot really grasp what your parents did by not doing anything for you.'

Mary: 'To tell the truth, my father was never at home; he never took care of my mother and of us, the kids. And you ask me to thank him for that. That's not logical. How can I thank someone for the things he has not done?'

Sheikh Aly: 'You said earlier that your parents gave you everything.'

Mary: 'I was thinking of my mum and not really of my dad. My mother was not there because she worked, and my father for other reasons.'

Sheikh Aly: 'Then you condemn your father?'

Mary: 'In a way…yes.'

Sheikh Aly: 'Nonetheless it is God who wanted it that way during your childhood. You received spiritual instruction that allowed you today to forge ahead and be independent thanks to both parents.'

Mary: 'It's hard for a girl of ten not to be able to rely on her father and to know that her mother must work all the time to fulfil the family's needs.'

Sheikh Aly: 'You have judged and condemned your father. But what you don't realise is that your mother appears to be an ideal model to you. Thanks to your father's behaviour! We end up marrying the parent whom we have condemned in order to reproduce our parents' relationship as we experienced it during childhood.'

Mary: 'You mean to say that I have unconsciously married my father?'

Sheikh Aly: 'That's it! But when we become aware that we have condemned and judged our parents through ignorance, we can come back to the judgement to change it into forgiveness. We have to understand the role of forgiveness in everything that we do. We have to remove all vices from our heart. Forgiveness allows us to achieve this objective. All the prophets without exception practised forgiveness. They responded to evil with good and they saw their enemies becoming their defenders.

'When you are moved by revenge, you put yourself in a situation where you suffer more. Forgiveness is important. We have to look at our parents as God's choice. They have given us the spiritual instruction that we were destined to receive from God in order to fulfil our role on earth. Sheikh Ahmadou Bamba wrote for his mother:

'God, don't ask her too many questions in her tomb, questions to which she won't find the answers. Be merciful to her.'

'So, we ask God for forgiveness for having judged our parents, but in addition to this we ask God to forgive them:

'God, please forgive our parents and be merciful towards them as they were towards us when we were young.'

'We hence remove all vices from our heart, and this will help us to be aware of the spiritual instruction that our parents have given us. When you conduct an assessment of your relationship with your parents, each time that you tell yourself that they have not done something for you, you should tell yourself that at the same time they educated your soul. From birth, they helped us to fight our desires, our bodily appetites, and guided our spiritual development. From the moment that we become aware of this, we are no longer in the dynamic of judgement. We reconsider our judgement, and we tell ourselves that actually our judgement was a mistake, and from now on we will abstain from it. The most important thing is to know what God wanted to teach us through the events in our lives.'

Mary: 'You are so noble…'

Sheikh Aly: 'You must forgive your husband Mary. And love him for God. Call him and ask for forgiveness and tell him that you love him. Ask him to come and see me.'

Some time later, it was Mary herself who called to arrange a meeting for Bob. Bob met Sheikh Aly late that evening. As soon as Sheikh Aly saw him, he asked him for news of Mary. Bob was happy because his wife had called him after months of silence. Sheikh Aly told Bob that he thought Mary loved him a lot. Bob smiled.

Sheikh Aly asked him why he and Mary had separated when they still felt so much love for each other.

Bob explained to Sheikh Aly that he had done everything to please his wife, but she was too demanding. Every time he went out to play sport or to see members of his family, Mary made a fuss. He added that Mary left the house because he did not want to celebrate their wedding anniversary.

Sheikh Aly asked Bob the reason why he refused to celebrate it. Bob had converted to Islam and said that since his conversion, he had decided not to celebrate any more anniversaries.

Sheikh Aly asked Bob if his parents celebrated their wedding anniversary.

Bob was shocked by the question. He explained that his father wanted to celebrate their anniversaries but his mother refused as she didn't like inviting people to their home. As a child, he didn't like his cousins coming to his house either because they disturbed him. Like his mother, he thought that inviting people to visit was a chore. Several times his father had forced his mother to celebrate anniversaries and his parents quarrelled a lot about the matter. Bob always took his mother's side.

Sheikh Aly then asked him if he refused to celebrate anniversaries because of his childhood experiences or because of Islam. Bob was perplexed. Then Sheikh Aly explained that he must go through an assessment of his parents' relationship and suggested that he make up with his wife.

Days later, Bob and Mary started a new married life. Mary understood that with Bob, she was re-experiencing her father's absences which she had strongly condemned in her childhood. As for Bob, he had become aware that his conversion had nothing to do with his hatred of family celebrations. By denying them to Mary, he was continuing to unconsciously support his mother while attributing the blame to his new religion. The couple has, thanks to Liberation Therapy, managed to begin a healthy relationship in their married life.

The examples given above suffice to show that the relationship problem is found in all countries, in all cultures. It is a universal problem. The most important thing is not collecting case histories but finding out how the mechanism works in order for release to take place.

We must realise that most of us are affected by the family relationship legacy that has been passed down through at least five generations. This means that those who succeed in freeing themselves from this burden will stop passing it on to their children, and after them, to all their descendants. Let us imagine the new society that will be born from their efforts to awaken their consciousness!

We cannot close this chapter without underlining the fact that there are as many situations as there are individuals coping with their family relationship legacy. Your own story would certainly be interesting…

CONCLUSION

At the end of this little book, we would like to draw our reader's attention to the fact that this is just a brief summary of what Liberation Therapy actually is. As we said in the introduction, it functions as a framework that can be adapted to each individual's life story.

It is important to stress that Liberation Therapy only enables us to understand the tortuous paths from our childhood and adolescence that have led us to live our present lives in contradiction to our intentions. The light that it brings is a real relief and proves that everything becomes possible the moment our awakened consciousness enables us to take control of our life again.

However, its power stops at this point. It is not

the Therapy that will lead us to the forgiveness that we have described and illustrated as the only liberator. Neither can it make the necessary efforts on our behalf to re-establish harmonious relationships nor heal us as if by magic from the old harmful and destructive reflexes.

Instead, the Therapy gives us back our liberty of action, along with our consciousness. It is up to us to assume this liberty and use its effects for it is through this work to transform ourselves that we rebuild ourselves. If we have a bad character, if we are jealous or violent, if we have a tendency towards negativity or destructive criticism, the fact that we know that all this springs from judgement and that we judged one of our parents will not change anything in our life if we do not voluntarily commit ourselves to work on our self-transformation.

Finally, we will add that Liberation Therapy is merely a step on the Initiatory Way to Peace defined by our school after extensive study of the life of Beings of Peace from different eras, cultures and faiths. The Initiatory Way to Peace consists of twelve steps and each of them relates to our inner life.

It is this work to transform ourselves that will let us discover the treasures and exceptional gifts that our childhood experiences have given us. While these are hidden under our fears, anger, impatience, jealousy, and passion for this material world, we will remain blind to the sun within us.

Why did the Beings of Peace have such exceptional destinies when nothing or nobody in their family predisposed them to this? (Most came from an ordinary background.)

Why it is that such-and-such a musician, writer or painter is able to discover the beauty of music, the elegance of poetry or appreciate the shimmer of colours in an impressionist scene when the rest of his family remains untouched?

When we get rid of our obstacles, which are merely the judgement and the condemnation that we have formulated, we are able to find our original nature composed of kindness, love, compassion and original faith. We are then able to open up to all the beauty that sings around us and we can see the joyous splendour of the divine in all that has been created.

Let us be convinced:

"Everything relating to human beings is internal. There is nothing, absolutely nothing, that is external to him."

It is this work of self-transformation that will enable us to metamorphose ourselves into a Being of Peace, a benefactor of humanity. It is this that will help us to reconstruct ourselves and confer not only the merit but also the powerful wisdom linked to this transformation. The founder of our school, Sheikh Ahmadou Bamba, used to say in this respect:

"There is no greater knowledge than the knowledge that teaches us our weaknesses and shortcomings..."

This knowledge is the essential condition for change. This change will allow us to create a more harmonious society that is based on the innermost being of each one of us. It will be a society respectful of itself, respectful of its environment, and respectful of all that populates it and gives it life. Such a society will be ready to establish and to live in the Golden Age.

If you wish to go further…

If you wish to pursue your quest for meaning and inner liberation, you will be pleased to know that we have training courses which can help you. Do not hesitate to contact us if you need additional information on Liberation Therapy and its different stages or our training courses for Inner Peace.

Below are the e-mail addresses of the different branches of our school:

Paris
contact_fra@international-sufi-school.org

London
sufi_school@yahoo.com

Reunion Island
contact_reunion@international-sufi-school.org

Senegal
contact_sn@international_sufi_school.org

Canada
contact_iss@yahoo.ca

Turkey
bahauddin_faqir@yahoo.com

Mauritius
mru_international_sufi_school@yahoo.com